Suddenly, Mexico!

by Katherine Hatch

Copyright © 2009 Katherine Hatch
All rights reserved.

ISBN: 1-4392-4585-1
EAN13: 9781439245859

Visit www.booksurge.com to order additional copies

Contents

Author's Note	
Foreword	
Flashback	1
Mirage?	5
Popocatepetl	7
Alma	11
Neighborhood Gossip	17
Padre Juan	21
A New Padre	23
Handyman	27
Stormy Weather	33
Newcomers	39
Cocktails, Anyone?	43
The Rich Are Different	49
Green Man	53
Let There Be Light	57
Music Of The Street	63
Good News	67
Uninvited Guest	69
Married Priest, Or Not?	77
Birdbrains	81
Fiesta	85
And Another Fiesta...	89
Living With The Day Of The Dead	91
"Discovering" Paraiso	95
Veracruz	97
Carlos	105
Bell Ringers (1)	107
Bell Ringers (2)	109
Spook Show	111
Max	117
Knowing Helen	125
Bulls	135
Three Healers	139
Last Call	153
Stroke of Luck	157
Heart To Heart	163
Something Like Woof! Woof!	165
Now And Then	167
The Shepherd	171

The imaginary village of Paraiso is spelled with an accent on the i, which is sounded in Spanish.

Since this book is written in English, Spanish readers may insert an imaginary accent mark in the name of the imaginary village.

The Author

Dedication

To Barb

Last night I heard music in a garden and laughter, and realized again how sweet life can be. It was a perfect night, with bright stars and the air perfumed by jasmine blooming on my wall. When I heard guitars and trumpets softly mellow at a neighbor's party, I wanted to wrap the music around me with the stars in the velvety night, and I thought again how lucky I am to live in Mexico.

Before I came to Mexico, I had no idea of what to expect. It was a new world for me, as though I had been living in black and white and suddenly my life was in color. I was bowled over. Even now, after four decades in this country of constant surprises, I catch my breath in wonder. The truth is, Mexico isn't like the United States. The only thing we have in common is the ugly gash of a border cutting off people on both sides and making everyone mad.

Flashback

I had always wanted to come to Mexico, and in the autumn of 1968, I followed my dream. I left Oklahoma and came to Mexico City as a foreign correspondent to write articles about the Olympic Games being held that October. The country was on holiday, playing host to the world, with thousands of colorful flags and peace doves fluttering in the sunshine. Eager tourists crowded every corner, marveling over the beauties of a land they had only imagined.

One day when three fellow reporters and I were discovering the Pink Zone, we paused at a corner to decide in which direction we wanted to continue. A tall concrete post blocked part of the sidewalk—I didn't notice what it was for—and I saw a teenager gluing a flimsy paper flyer of some kind to the post. I read it. It invited everyone to a rally at the Plaza of the Three Cultures where a strike would be suspended. That was all I got with my basic Spanish; I missed the meaning.

We talked about going to the rally, but the day was so lovely, with soft breezes and bright sunshine, and we had already filed stories at the Communications Tower for the next day's papers, that we decided to skip it and go, instead, for a long, leisurely lunch at a restaurant someone had told us about. It was overlooking a lake in Chapultepec Park and it served caviar and icy Russian vodka, unavailable in the United States in those days. Our decision may have

SUDDENLY, MEXICO!

saved our lives. The sun had set on a delightful day when waiters called us a taxi and we returned to our rooms at the Hotel Montejo on Paseo de la Reforma. Surprisingly, all night long and into the waking hours of the dawn, the sound of sirens filled our heads.

The next morning I asked the Bell Captain about them. He mumbled something about students, *los estudiantes*, and hurried away from me.

That autumn of 1968 became famous for its rage and riots around the world. People of all ages and nationalities were taking to the streets to protest against things they didn't like about their governments. In Mexico, rebellion swept from university classrooms to tree-lined boulevards as citizens by the thousands made their voices heard, demanding the truth in newspapers, open meetings by the government, and removal of the long-ruling political party's iron fist from their lives. To those in power, rebellion meant war.

Ten days before the opening ceremonies of the Olympic Games, leaders of antigovernment demonstrations held a mass meeting in Mexico City to declare a moratorium on their protests for the duration of the Games. It was the rally we had skipped. Minutes after the "truce" was announced, snipers fired into the festive crowd in the Plaza of the Three Cultures. Mexico's one-party political system collapsed in a rain of bullets, victim of the massacre it had engineered. In the days ahead, as the country buried its dead, it struggled to emerge as a modern nation.

When my assignment ended, I wanted to know everything about Mexico. I went back to Oklahoma, quit my newspaper job and sold my house. Through friends,

FLASHBACK

I rented a Mexican *casita* for as long as I wanted to stay. It was in a village called Paraiso, which means paradise, near Cuernavaca, the "City of Eternal Springtime." I had learned the worst of Mexico, the Tlatelolco massacre. I wanted to discover the best.

✲ ✲ ✲

Mirage?

I crossed the border at Laredo, Texas, and headed south down the two-lane highway. I was fascinated by the life I passed in villages and little town squares that looked like dusty clusters of the building blocks I had played with as a child. Men were riding burros down dirt roads while their women and children walked beside them. At one point, I had to stop where twenty men were working on the highway, laborers in their undershirts and dirty cotton pants, worn-out shoes on their feet, digging with picks and shovels to widen the road. I thought I knew enough Spanish to ask if I could drive around them, but no one seemed to understand me. I waited. A worker stuck his smiling face in my car's open window and asked, "You go?" He pointed toward a mirage of tall buildings, only it wasn't a mirage. In the crystal air, Mexico City had popped into view.

"*Si, si,*" I said eagerly.

He stepped back, barked an order and waved a red rag. I gunned the motor, anxious to be off.

I passed little traffic and only a few towns set back from the highway. Rays of the afternoon sun bounced off fleecy clouds as I swooped down a hill in a beautiful green meadow and saw a shepherd. He was a boy of eleven or twelve, sitting on a grassy bank ignoring the flock of sheep scattered around him while he looked out toward the highway. He held a small transistor radio to his ear. Even speeding past, I recognized it as a Sony. I had one like it.

The shepherd caught my eye, and then I was gone and he was gone.

Since that day, I've thought many times about "my shepherd." Like countless generations of Mexicans, he had been isolated on his hillside until someone put the transistor radio into his hands and he suddenly was tuned to the world. He would never be the same again, nor would Mexico.

✼ ✼ ✼

Popocatepetl

I live in Paraiso, a village in a high mountain valley amid spectacular peaks of the Sierra Madre range and with the best climate on earth. My house is at the lower end of a deep pine forest that rolls down a thousand feet to the *tierra caliente* of the Tropic of Cancer, where palm trees crackle in the wind and barefoot boys cultivate roses by the mile.

There are only two seasons in Paraiso: rainy and dry. On the rare occasions that I feel sentimental about my snowy Midwestern childhood, I go to the freezer and place my hand on top of the ice cube tray until I can no longer endure it. Then I return to the fireplace and throw another cube in the wine. I light the fireplace in January or February, when the temperature drops to sixty degrees. The rest of my year is blue skies, or rain that falls straight down.

My house is simple, built of adobe bricks with a red tile roof and large windows. It has two bedrooms and a studio with a sleeping loft, a fireplace for January, a Pullman kitchen, living and dining spaces with glorious views, and a small swimming pool and garden off a covered stone terrace. The view on all sides is of the mountains crowned with a pair of snowcapped volcanoes, Popocatepetl and Ixtaccihuatl. Friends and I used to take picnics of gin martinis and cold fried chicken to the volcanoes on sunny days. We took bags of potato chips, too, but wild horses ripped open the sacks one year and ate all of them. We didn't quit going; we just quit taking potato chips. "The Rowdy Crowd," we were called, and whenever we could all get together, we took picnic excursions, hiking up to Popo's crater in the crunchy snow, throwing snowballs and swapping stories while the bright sun and biting wind stung our faces.

Those times ended one night in December 1994, when Popo erupted with a roar and a mighty sound-and-light show. Neighbors and I walked a block from my house to stand on a low hill and watch flying sparks and molten lava running down the volcano's slopes. This was the most exciting thing that had ever happened to people who lived near the volcanoes, and they resisted when frightened soldiers in Jeeps told them to get out. They didn't want to leave home and were afraid the soldiers would steal their meager possessions. Eventually, the government gave both volcanoes their own twenty-four-hour television channel for all of the people who wouldn't believe Popo really had erupted until they saw it on television.

On the morning I discovered the bottom of my garden pool etched with millions of tiny black ashes, I realized that everything I had thought about the "picturesque" volcanoes had changed in a heartbeat. I'm not saying I'm afraid of them, but I haven't packed a picnic basket since.

My friends and I found other amusements: playing charades, rain or shine; floating down the river at Las Estacas in water so clean we could read the print on the beer-bottle caps in the riverbed. The river ended in a huge natural pool where we swam through an underwater

POPOCATEPETL

spring that bubbled to the surface like Old Faithful. We explored and swam in Lake Tequesquitengo a few times, but the *jejenes*—extraordinarily hungry, invisible bugs with the worst habits of chiggers, mosquitoes, and red ants—chased us away.

* * *

Alma

A few days after I settled into my house, I bought it. I knew in my heart that I would stay. My next-door neighbor, Alma, introduced herself to me as the wife of Don Angel, the Paraiso mayor. She invited me to her house for a glass of *agua de Jamaica,* a popular hot-weather beverage made from boiled hibiscus flowers. I accepted. When I arrived, her husband was going to work and we hurriedly shook hands as he went out the door.

Don Angel and Alma's small house was neat and clean, with no frills; three bedrooms, a living-dining room with two sofas and five wooden chairs, a tiny kitchen, and a bath. I had a problem with how to address Alma. Was she, as the wife of Paraiso's mayor, his *esposa?* Or his woman, *mujer?* Was there a difference? Here was my big chance to make friends with a Mexican and I didn't have a clue what to call her. So I settled on *Señora.*

Having a Mexican friend is something foreigners earn, like a merit badge or sainthood. It is bestowed status, not easily won and certainly not passed around. Because I was living in Mexico, it was logical that I made friends with Mexicans, but it wasn't easy. They already had their friends and families, several generations happily entertaining themselves. I had my friends and families, too, but most of them were living in another country.

All of the hundreds of foreign residents I came to know in Paraiso over the years seemed to have a Mexican friend who advised him or her on all "important" matters, including, but not restricted to, the weather, dentists, the best tamales, uses for bee pollen, and remedies for scorpion stings. The advice was not always correct, nor was it always wrong, but because Mexicans fervently believed they were experts on everything, they loved their role, and the advice cost nothing.

I cleared my throat. "Alma," I said, "may I call you Alma?"

"*Si*," she said with a warm smile. "And you are Kate?" She gave it the Spanish pronunciation: "Kat." I smiled and nodded. She was solid, not given to fat, five feet tall, with an angular bronze face and large brown eyes that looked straight through me. She wore a short-sleeved cotton dress under her bib apron, and tennis shoes. Her black hair was woven into two thick braids that reached her waist.

Every morning after fixing her family's early breakfast of coffee with milk and sweet rolls, Alma rode a noisy, rusting bus to the market where she sat all day on the cement floor, selling herbs she had grown in her garden. She arranged them in little mounds like pyramids in front of her on a busy aisle, and stayed until late afternoon, when she returned home to prepare the big meal of the day for Don Angel and their children: Carlos, the youngest at ten; a daughter, Blanca, twelve; and Angelito, thirteen.

Alma told me that, as a teenager, Don Angel was already six feet tall and brawny, working on offshore Mexican oil rigs. He was good at the work, and by the time he was twenty and they were married, he was a supervisor. The next year, he quit to become Paraiso's mayor, but he never lost the rolling walk of a seafaring man tossed up on shore. Four generations of his family had lived on the same plot of ground two doors from my house, and in each generation, the oldest son was Paraiso's mayor. The first to serve as mayor had been Don Angel's great-grandfather, appointed by President Porfirio Diaz at the dawn of the twentieth century. Don Angel's grandfather held the largely ceremonial job until he died in bed with his *mujer* when he was seventy. Next, Don Angel's father was given the job, but a shooting accident passed the job to Don Angel when he was twenty-one. The title, "Don," went with the job as a show of respect; the job didn't pay enough to make anyone want to hold it without having some kind of extra advantage.

There wasn't much to being Mayor of Paraiso. The village had four policemen, but no fire department nor water department, nor city hall. Most of the time, Don Angel roamed around in his polished black cowboy boots, white guayabera, and creased black trousers, and he never left home without his straw hat from Michoacan with a tassel down the back. He settled disputes between neighbors and gave his official blessing to weddings and fiestas. He was a peace-loving man, but some citizens took exception to his duty to maintain order during fiestas, so he wore his hat to remind everyone that only a really tough *hombre* was man enough to wear a hat with tassels.

Our conversation paused. "I want to tell you about the village of Paraiso," Alma said, excitement building in her voice for the story forming in her head. "It isn't like any other place. It has always been known for its special feeling that attracts people. Even strangers notice that it has *alma*. That means 'soul.' Everyone senses that the village is charmed.

"That's why we've had so many famous visitors. They came for the climate, and the *alma*: El Conquistador Hernan Cortes, Emperor Maximilian of Hapsburg, the Empress Carlota, La India Bonita—the girlfriend of Maximilian." She paused for a breath. "Those are the most famous—except for Emiliano Zapata, of course, but he was from around here, a local horse trainer."

"What did they do here?"

Alma laughed. "What everyone does—make love or make money or make trouble. There wasn't a lot to do if they didn't work the land. There still isn't. The town's red-light district was around here. I'm sure some residents and visitors familiarized themselves with it. That's something most of our neighbors don't want to talk about, but it's the truth. In the old days, people had to ford a river to reach Paraiso," Alma continued. "Lovers, always hardy souls, didn't mind because the village was so romantic, with its ancient trees and a hush in the air like faraway music. People brought their picnics and homemade raspberry wine and stayed until they could see the moon. They would listen to palm trees blowing in the wind, inhale the aroma of the eucalyptus trees, smell sweet orange blossoms and jasmine as they wandered through the meadows of wildflowers. In springtime, flowering wild trees bloomed on the hillsides, their soft colors bright against the brown earth—lavender *jacarandas,* yellow and pink *primaveras.* It is still a magical place."

"*Estas de acuerdo* (Do you agree)?" I asked her.

"*Absolutamente.* By the time the ladies of the night found a quieter place, Maximilian and Carlota were long gone," Alma continued. "A few tired old prostitutes were here into the 1950s, waving forlornly to customers from tiny windows in their cribs on the street of the penitentiary. They didn't know they were waving goodbye until police moved them out of town...but not very far out of town.

"Paraiso never pretended to be more than a small village. That hasn't changed, although almost all of the old families are gone. Today's fancy folk are mostly second or third generation who came after the Revolution."

She paused. "Have you noticed the fruit trees in bloom? Every year at this time we have the most miraculous gift of flowering trees which no one else can see in our 'hidden orchard.'" She turned in her chair to rest her eyes upon the trees. I followed her gaze. Smooth boughs bore bright white and peach-colored fruit blossoms glowing against a background of shaggy, stiff strips of gray and rust-colored bark on the eucalyptus trees. I reached to touch a blossom; the petals were so soft they were barely there.

"In the fading days of the Revolution, one of Zapata's troops, a boy, discovered this garden. Legend says it was Zapata himself who ordered the boy to protect it, which he did. Around him the fields were in flames, towns and villages destroyed, the sugarcane and corn, all of the crops were burned to the ground, but the hidden orchard and the boy survived. After the Revolution, he built a little hut here in the wilderness and lived out his life as protector of the hidden orchard."

"That's a lovely story," I said. "Can you tell me about those old eucalyptus trees?" I had admired them since the first day I smelled their pungent aroma and saw them towering over a small church near my house.

"They were planted by the Emperor Maximilian," Alma said. "He wanted an *allèe* leading to his summerhouse. A hundred and fifty years later, only a few of the trees remain, but the summerhouse is still here. For many years it was a ruin, with a rusted metal sign warning passersby it was federal property and to stay away. Weeds and tall grasses ran rampant and no one ventured in except neighborhood boys playing soccer.

"I have heard rumors that someone wants to make a garden, and that would be nice, but you know, the government..." She shrugged her shoulders. The summerhouse stands today on a little clearing in the old garden. It's known officially as the State Botanical Garden, but neighbors call it "Maximilian's Garden."

※ ※ ※

Neighborhood Gossip

Alma had told me that the little stone church of San Miguel Arcangel was one of the first churches in Mexico, built in the early 1500s by El Conquistador Hernan Cortes, and that my house was built originally for an aide-de-camp of the Emperor Maximilian in the mid-1800s. I find it comfortable to live with history. There is no sense of competition with your neighbors when half of the people you know live in antique, if not historical, houses. A neighbor lives in a former stable of Cortes's soldiers. Another's house was a way station for the mule-drawn wagons and carriages that hauled gold and silver, fresh fruit, and sugarcane on the cobblestone and mud roads between Veracruz and Acapulco when Mexico had the main route to both the Atlantic and Pacific Oceans.

Neither "El Conquistador" Hernan Cortes nor the Emperor Maximilian of Hapsburg was made especially welcome here. They were humored, endured, obeyed or not, seen as part of a procession of foreigners who have come seeking riches, fame, revolution, or sunshine, and have fallen under Mexico's spell.

Cortes, who ordered his ships burned so no one could leave after he made landfall near Veracruz, ended his career with his own palace in Cuernavaca. It's still here, a museum now, second in Mexico only to the renowned National Museum of Anthropology. One of the most amazing displays is the armor his soldiers wore. How small they must have been! Three hundred men were all he had, and around a dozen horses. The horses won the day for him; local people had never seen a horse and the little equines of Cortes's era didn't have to be as big as Man O' War to be scary.

Maximilian had horses, too, but he didn't depend on them to subdue anyone. He had believed the people who had told him that Mexico wanted him for its emperor, so he and the Empress Carlota, his grumpy wife, set sail from their mansion overlooking the sea in Trieste, anxious for their victorious journey to Mexico. But when they arrived in the port of Veracruz, ready to be welcomed and cheered, no one was there. No bands, no flowers, nobody. As the horses pulling their royal carriage scrambled up the steep stone slope at the harbor, the only sounds were the clatter of horses' hooves and the slamming of doors as the Veracruzanos voted "No!" on the foreign emperor. He didn't last long. Benito Juarez, a once and future heroic president of Mexico, saw to that: firing squad for Maximilian.

A month after I moved into my house, an investigator from the National Anthropology and History Institute, called INAH, knocked on my door. "I have been told that yours is an historic house," he said. "For the record, could you tell me how old it is?"

He was young and eager, carrying a clipboard and a shiny pen. I had work to do in my garden. One of my rules for a long, happy life was, "Beware of eager young men with clipboards."

Alma had already warned me that in an extreme case INAH could declare a property to be a "cultural heritage" and confiscate it for the government, even when someone was living in it. In simpler cases, a homeowner could be forbidden from making structural changes without the Institute's permission. I decided to lie.

"I don't know exactly how old this little house is, but it isn't historic. It's just old." I smiled as he thanked me and I shut the door. "One hundred and fifty years old," I said, under my breath.

The little church of San Miguel Arcangel was built about the same time as the Cuernavaca Cathedral in the 1520s. The style of the little church made clear its age and serious purpose. It was not built with bingo in mind. There were few distractions for the faithful, and no dramatic embellishments. It was simple and plain, spare to the point of punishment, meant for the conversion of heathens. Wooden pews formed stiff rows on either side of the center aisle—women on one side, men on the other—and kneeling boards were hardwood, not sissy, squishy cushions. A stone altar, unadorned except for a costumed statue of San Miguel Arcangel wielding his sword and a painted depiction of Jesus, commanded attention at the front. A parishioner told me that empty niches on the side walls once held statues of saints, but they were long gone. The last to disappear was San Francisco, still wearing his scratchy brown cassock and holding a small, poorly stuffed bluebird in his hand.

Over time, San Miguel Arcangel became a favorite church of ambassadors and counts, European royalty, Mexican philosophers, and Spanish artists who built their beautiful villas around it because they loved this village and wanted to be prayed over by friends and buried in Paraiso. Hundreds of roses adorning the tiny church from entry to belfry and heavenly music by a string quartet in the choir loft were within the reach of Padre Juan, the local priest, who was looked upon by all of Paraiso as "a treasure."

✻ ✻ ✻

Padre Juan

He lived in a small dark space at the back of the church, more an afterthought than a room, with a cot, a good lamp for reading, a straight-backed wooden chair, a wedge of closet, a small bathroom, and his books overflowing a low shelf, stacked and scattered on the floor. Padre Juan's room was next to a dispensary, where twice a week he met with neighbors who couldn't afford to be sick and treated them with medicines donated by wealthy hypochondriacs who didn't want to get well.

He was a rare man, practicing what he preached, with a gentle, round face and a humble manner. He ate one meal a day and a bowl of broth at night, delivered by the Comida Corrida take-out up the street, a five-table café with a cement floor known by its regular customers as the "*Canina Corrida*," or "running dog," because of the two street dogs that set their alarms to its daily opening.

Having spent twenty years as a papal linguist in the Vatican, Padre Juan believed it was important to speak to every soul in its own language, "the better to help them in the hereafter." Most mornings, after his prayers, he read his Bible, and then he spent an hour or two studying a language he didn't know before he opened his daily newspaper to see if he had won the lottery. It was a measure of his faith that he always expected to win, but he never blamed God for the fact that he didn't. He knew God wasn't choosing the numbers.

At the end of Padre Juan's food chain was a plate of scraps he scrounged daily from neighbors for Lobo and

Canelo, the two mongrel dogs that watched over Paraiso. As is common with many couples, one dog had more character than his partner. With a grizzled muzzle, large brown eyes, and a deep chest crossed by scars, Lobo met life with a bright gaze and an eager step. His pale yellow pal Canelo had his own style, and trotted along with one ear folded over halfway, peering down his nose at every crack in the sidewalk. Still, he was excellent at following Lobo and made the best of his Sancho Panza role in life.

✹ ✹ ✹

A New Padre

I was exploring my neighborhood a few days after I met Padre Juan when I saw people standing outside the church. I hadn't heard the church bells ring and I was curious about the crowd, so I crossed the street. My neighbors standing in the open church doors looked perplexed. Don Angel and Alma waved, and then Don Angel walked over to shake hands and introduce himself to me again. He was frowning, as though storm clouds were passing overhead.

"What is it?" I asked.

Alma shook her head, puzzled.

"A new padre." Don Angel nodded toward the doors. "He seems to be *loco*."

"Why do you think he's crazy?" I asked.

Don Angel forced a laugh. "He wants to stop us from our fiestas! Change our lives! He said he has a moral code for us, and every Mexican will live in a sober and moral state."

"What state is that?" Alma asked.

"No state I want to live in," Don Miguel replied, winking as he slipped his arm around his wife's waist.

Alma had told me that, at any given moment, half of the parishioners disagreed with the other half. They were divided between those who wanted to share "the Peace," hug, and sing the Mass in Spanish, and people who wanted the Mass in Latin with no singing, no hugging, and with the men and women on separate sides of the aisle, where God intended them to sit.

In past years, disagreements over these differences with one priest or another had become so heated the police were called, even though no one in Mexico ever wanted to call the police.

"They are nothing but *ratones*," Alma declared with a violent shake of her head. She paused to laugh at herself. "We Mexicans are crazy sometimes."

At that moment, a man's loud voice boomed through the church: "Don't touch that woman!"

It so startled Don Angel that he released his arm from his wife's waist and looked over his shoulder to see who had shouted.

"Yes, you!" came the voice again. It was a priest Don Angel had never seen, tall and heavy and bald, with a puffy red face. "Who are you?" the priest demanded as he stomped to the doors. He wore a somber black suit and an ornate cross around his neck that was suspended on a black cord thick enough for a gallows. "Is this man bothering you?" he asked Alma in his loud voice.

She giggled. "Oh no, Padre. He's my husband."

"You are a new padre?" Don Angel asked.

"*Sí*, Señor, Padre Julio. Julio Cesar. I have come here to assist your Padre Juan and to reform the people."

"We don't need reforming," Don Angel said, "and we don't need anyone besides Padre Juan. He is our priest."

"And you might be—"

"I am Don Angel Mendez, Presidente Municipal of Paraiso, defender of the faith and of the Mexican Constitución." He removed his hat and tipped it before continuing. "I don't know you well, Padre Julio. I have heard of you. You may call me Don Angel." He extended a large, leathery hand in greeting and the priest touched it with a smooth white hand. His fidgeting fingers looked like squirming white mice.

Don Angel stepped forward. "And this is my wife, Doña Alma."

The new priest bowed slightly and Alma nodded in what she hoped was a sign of respect, but the new padre's silence irritated Don Angel.

"I have heard of you," Padre Julio said sharply. "You're one of the leaders of the fiestas."

"*Si*, Señor. As Presidente Municipal, it's my duty to oversee our fiestas. Our fiesta to San Miguel Arcangel is famous throughout Mexico for its parades and fireworks and the Chinelo dancers."

"And for the drinking," Padre Julio interrupted, "pulque, tequila, beer…"

Thinking he might soften the new padre, Don Angel said, "But Padre, you wouldn't expect us to celebrate with dry throats."

"We'll see about that," Padre Julio said sharply. At that moment, Padre Juan emerged from the church and, seeing the others, walked toward them.

"How can our Chinelos dance for six consecutive hours in their heavy costumes without cool libations?" Don Angel called.

We all watched Padre Julio stop and turn around. "Very easily," he said. "They can sit down and rest. Or maybe we'll have to get rid of the dancers?"

"Get rid of the Chinelos?" Don Angel shouted, stunned that the traditional dancers might be benched. "*Loco*," he muttered to Alma and me.

Padre Julio turned on his heel and hurried to the church.

"Did I hear correctly?" Padre Juan asked Don Angel. "This new padre is talking about 'reforms' and getting rid of the Chinelos? We must all be strong. God is testing us!"

* * *

Handyman

A week later, I awoke one morning to a rooster crowing and barely had my eyes open when I heard someone pounding on my gate. I hurried barefoot to peek out the little "spy" window cut into the door, but I saw no one.

"*Si?*" I asked. "Who is it?"

I peered in every direction, but didn't see anyone until I stretched to my full five feet nine inches and looked down. A solemn little kid was staring up at me.

"*Buenos dias*, Señora," he chirped as I opened the gate. He wore faded black shorts, a white T-shirt, and old black high-top tennis shoes. His hair was parted and slicked down. He kept staring. I asked him what he wanted.

He introduced himself as Carlos-your-neighbor and said he was the younger son of the mayor. His mother had sent him to help me in the garden. He was ten years old and said he could work all morning. He went to school in the afternoon.

I glanced at my garden: a dozen flowering plants had fallen over dead in their pots; heaps of dried leaves lay in the grass; waterlogged palm fronds filled the pool. Only the grass didn't need attention; it was dead.

"Maybe I can work for you?" he asked in a timid voice.

"You're hired, Carlos," I said. "How much?"

He shrugged his shoulders and held up two fingers.

"Two pesos it is, Carlos." We shook hands. He had a little boy's hands and voice, but he rolled his *r*'s, affecting an adult attitude of great importance.

To me, hiring Carlos was like buying insurance on my house, my pets, and my peace of mind. Although he was ten years old, he was small for his age. His job was to tend my small garden, watering during the dry season, sweeping leaves and fallen blossoms out of the grass and flower beds every day with a long, feathery straw broom. He skimmed the pool and carried out trash. This last task, which he seemed to have trouble remembering, was the most important.

"It is not smart to store trash very long in a tropical climate," I told Carlos one day for the third time. With trash barrels in a closet in the garage, and the garage next to my studio, I had no leeway, odor-wise or furry-creature-wise, when something that should have been shut in a trash can wasn't. I explained it as simply as I could. Carlos finally understood. He not only gathered the trash, he dragged the big metal trash barrel out to the street every time he heard the grinding gears and the clanging cowbell of the trash truck heading our way.

He became my guide. He led me to the *tortilleria* for a kilo of fresh tortillas, then to La California, an open-air stand selling fruits and vegetables in season and firecrackers at Christmas. Next to it, a hole-in-the-wall grocery offered asparagus, strawberries, zucchini, and the freshest long-stemmed roses I had ever seen. At ten pesos a dozen—equivalent to eighty U.S. cents—they were an affordable luxury.

HANDYMAN

Our next stop was La Esperanza, Paraiso's tiny general store and informal social center, the place to exchange news or gossip while buying fresh sweet rolls for breakfast. All day and into the night, people gathered there to talk while they shopped or spent a minute out of the sun or rain, drinking a Coke or a Nehi or a bottle of tepid Victoria beer. Only a few customers could fit inside and still leave space for someone dashing in to buy an egg for breakfast or an aspirin for a sick child.

For people without a refrigerator, as most of Paraiso's residents were, La Esperanza was a lifeline of necessities. Every pueblo in Mexico had a store like La Esperanza; some bigger, some smaller, whatever the owner could afford. It had no door, only a corrugated metal shutter on the street, which the owner raised in the morning in time for schoolchildren's breakfasts and tugged down and locked each night after the last weary laborer passed on his way home. Guadalupe, or Lupe, as the owner was called, was a trim twenty-three-year-old with large, expressive eyes, curly hair, and a joyful personality. She was widowed at twenty, got over it, and inherited a tiny property from her husband, who had been a humorless accountant. Lupe built the *tienda* on her property and had opened for business a year before I arrived in Paraiso. She had been earning her own money ever since, while happily spending her days with the neighbors, including Rodrigo the curly-haired mechanic whose yard, with its enormous bougainvillea bush, was home to the dogs, Lobo and Canelo.

A bare bulb hung from the *tienda* ceiling between a small refrigerator and a rack of little bags of chips.

It carved a patch of light upon shelves crowded with tiny cans of tomatoes, chilies, and sauces, little bags of beans and rice and soups, the smallest possible loaves of white bread, individual waxed cartons of juice, and boxes of milk with a three-month shelf life. The light bulb cast its glow above the evening sidewalk where conversation flowed. Spoken this way among friends in the fading day, the Spanish language was all music and oaths, pleasantries and tawdry tales, and always spiced with laughter.

Adolescent boys lounged across the street, leaning against the back wall of the church. They laughed too loud and yelled and punched each other while they sneaked looks at the young girls who stood obediently silent beside their mothers outside the store. On summer nights, the boys played soccer in the street while the girls watched them and whispered behind their hands.

Because Paraiso was rimmed by mountains, there was no twilight. Night fell in a blink after a luminous orange and blue sunset spread across the sky like a painter's canvas. As soon as everyone filed out of the store, Guadalupe pulled down the shutter with a sharp rattling noise and people began their good nights: *buena noche* and *hasta mañana* were repeated like prayers, with *que le vaya bien* added as an affectionate afterthought.

Footfalls crunched over bits of gravel in the street; someone scuffed a pop bottle cap and it rolled with a tinny, wavering sound disappearing in the distance. Then the neighborhood would be silent until dawn, unless a stranger walked through and all the dogs woke up barking. Only when the unfamiliar footfalls died away could we go back to sleep.

HANDYMAN

My first day with Carlos, I bought a kilo of eggs, each egg carefully examined by Guadalupe and sold separately; a hundred grams of sugar in a brown paper sack, a kilo of coffee, a couple of ripe mangos, and a half dozen *cuernitos,* warm soft rolls beneath a golden crust, shaped like the horns on a bull. Carlos had eaten an early breakfast at home—sweet roll and coffee with milk—and he asked for a banana as we left the *tienda.*

Two white butterflies, each as big as my hand, floated above us like handkerchiefs, picking a path through the trees and flowers that lined our way. At the gate, they flew over the wall into my garden.

"A white butterfly in the garden is the spirit of someone who was happy there," Carlos announced.

"Who told you that?" I liked the idea and had never heard it.

"My mamá told me. She knows everything," he replied.

"Your mamá is wise," I said.

Carlos finished the banana as we stepped inside the gate. He threw the peel on the ground.

I said, "Carlos, please don't throw the banana peel on the ground. Lady Bird Johnson would be upset with you."

He picked up the banana peel. "Who is she?"

"She's a lady in Texas who doesn't like trash."

"OK," Carlos sighed, crushing the banana peel in his small hand. He threw it into the trash barrel.

※ ※ ※

Stormy Weather

On the first Sunday in August, Padre Julio Cesar made his official appearance before San Miguel's congregation.

It would be charitable to say he overwhelmed his parishioners with eloquence, but that wasn't exactly the truth. The truth was, before he had said five words people were holding their hands over their ears to shut out his whining, nasal tone. His listeners assumed he was a foreigner from Monterrey, or another faraway country, and that he didn't carry Paraiso around in his head the way they did. Whatever, he was odd and sounded strange and too loud, but after five minutes most people weren't listening anyway. He could have yelled, "Fire! Fire!" and only about half of them would have noticed, it being Sunday, after all, and yawns all around.

Don Angel and Alma were sitting halfway back in the church with their children. Don Angel's chin had already dropped as his eyes like pools of oil fluttered shut. That was the moment Padre Julio Cesar chose to catch the attention of everyone.

"I was talking with my new friend, your mayor, Don Angel, this week and we spoke of the coming fiesta of San Miguel," Padre Julio whined. "Don Angel told me about your dancers. What do you call them?"

"Chinelos!" a dozen voices shouted! A little buzz of energy was let loose in the church, as though maybe Padre Julio Cesar would be tolerable if he wanted to know about the Chinelos.

"Odd name," Padre Julio Cesar mumbled, loud enough for all to hear, and the corners of his mouth drooped. "Whoever they are, they will be banned from the San Miguel festivities if they insist on drinking alcohol. There will be no alcoholic beverages. No exceptions."

He made a quick sign of the cross and sat down to stare at his shoes.

Padre Juan stirred in his chair near the altar but didn't speak. He was accustomed to being second-string, the backup padre. The silence seemed to last forever, a vacuum of disbelief until voices broke out.

"No dancing at the fiestas? The man is insane!"

"No alcohol!"

"He will never last…"

Murmurs raced up the aisle to erupt in a chorus of "No! No!" rolling out from the altar. Children playing in the churchyard thought the cries were at them and they ran home as fast as they could.

It was no coincidence that the most elaborate fiesta of the year was to be held in the streets of Paraiso in one month. Everyone looked to it to redeem themselves with praying and penance for whatever idiotic, unmentionable acts they had committed during the year. No one believed Padre Julio Cesar would keep his sinister pledge. No alcohol? No Chinelos? What was the world coming to?

The following Sunday he elaborated.

"There is too much drinking during the fiestas," he said. "I have been called to stop it. The dancers and musicians must entertain us without entering an inebriated state. This is the first rule of my moral code.

One day, everyone in Mexico will live in a completely sober and moral state. Even your Chinelos."

When the church bells began ringing, parishioners hurried out to talk about the new padre and how to derail his plan. Surely, he realized how important the fiesta was. Without something to drink, how could people dance or march the long hours required to show their faithfulness to San Miguel?

"To do less would be sinful," muttered Don Angel. "What kind of priest threatens Chinelo dancers with banishment? They're only dancing, for God's sake! What has happened to our church? Doesn't the new padre know we have been raising toasts to the gods since before the Catholics arrived?"

A pall fell over the village. People who were customarily joyous at the approach of San Miguel's fiesta became lethargic and ill-tempered. Menacing clouds rumbled and tinted the sky purple. A chill wind blew roof tiles off houses. Men started fistfights. Women screamed at each other in the street. Babies cried all day. Dogs barked all night. Nothing was right.

Don Angel received a procession of villagers at his house; a few at first, then a steady flow of troubled souls knocking on his door, asking him to save the Chinelo dancers, save the fiesta.

"Padre Julio Cesar must understand that this is our religion," croaked Tio Gonzalo, the town's oldest inhabitant, who had dragged his skinny body on twisted legs to Don Angel's door. "The Chinelos carry the spirit of the fiesta," said Guadalupe, who had closed her *tienda* to join the crowd outside Don Angel's house.

Farmers, horsemen, beauticians and butchers, Rodrigo the curly-haired mechanic, customers from the Comida Corrida—dozens of people waited their turns at Don Angel and Alma's neat little cement block house to speak with Don Angel about saving the fiesta. Some shook his hand, some embraced him in an *abrazo,* some patted him on the back before scurrying out. The last person in line was Rodrigo. He greeted Don Angel and said he had been thinking about the problem.

"Over the centuries, our ancestors have celebrated San Miguel Arcangel thousands of times," he said. "We always pray to him before his fiesta and every year, without fail, he advises us: Dance, pray, laugh. Celebrate the glory."

Don Angel laughed. Of course he knew the yearly tradition; praying for advice, receiving it, always the same advice: Dance. Pray. Laugh. Celebrate the glory.

"We'll do the same this year. Just because there is a new priest doesn't mean we have to give up our traditions!" Rodrigo said, loudly enough for everyone to hear, and the crowd outside Don Angel's house let out a lusty cheer.

A week later, Padre Juan called together a group after Mass for what he said was "an important announcement." I was included; I don't know why. But by then I had lived in Mexico long enough that I had quit asking why about anything.

"We have a sacred duty to God and San Miguel Arcangel to adhere to our ancient tradition," Padre Juan said. "This doesn't mean drinking until you're sick, getting drunk for no good reason. We have good reasons: our heritage, our history, our fiesta demand it of us."

"What about Padre Julio Cesar?" Don Angel asked.

Padre Juan raised his index finger to hold our attention. "Not to worry," he said. "I have been praying about him. I have a highly placed contact in the cathedral in Mexico City. All will be well. Vayan con Dios."

✯ ✯ ✯

Newcomers

Most churchgoers walked home after the Mass, but a few of us foreigners who had been summoned by Padre Juan looked at one another in silence until I said I thought we were neighbors.

I had noticed that two of the men in the padre's group had been speaking Spanish and English, so I smiled and introduced myself as we left the churchyard. The shorter man, Diego, had a compact, husky physique, brown hair and mustache, and soft brown eyes. His partner, Santiago, was thinner and over six feet tall, with long fingers, silver hair, and light blue eyes that crinkled at the corners when he smiled. Both had been born in the United States to Mexican mothers; their fathers had contributed the dual citizenship.

Diego looked handsomely North African and Santiago had an aristocratic Spanish appearance. Put another way, Santiago looked more like an American or a Canadian and Diego might have been from the Middle East, the Midwest, or in between. In white Mexican guayaberas with white slacks and leather sandals, they could have been from anyplace.

"I grew up in a town so small the bus didn't stop unless someone flagged it down," Diego said by way of introduction. "I used to hear it gunning its motor through town at night and I swore someday I would ride it out of Minnesota. That's basically what I did," he grinned. "I worked with the Arab-American organizations at the United Nations and my coworkers always thought I was one of them—regardless of their home countries."

Santiago's mother was Basque and his grandfather was French. He had been a U.S. banker in the Americas until Fidel Castro kicked him out of Cuba.

"That's when I began to plan my retirement," he said. "I had to leave everything behind and the Cuban government didn't send my property until five years later. Eventually, I received everything except a couple of bottles of Johnny Walker Black I was saving for a farewell party. I guess those went to Fidel."

"How did you get out of Cuba?" I asked.

"Foreign bankers were called in by the government and told we would have to get out. The Cuban officials were polite; they gave me ten days to leave the country and a one-way ticket to Miami. The bank headquarters in New York wired money to Miami for me so I wouldn't be broke when I got to the States."

"So there wasn't a farewell party," Diego said, brown eyes laughing.

"Speaking of parties, was that mariachi I heard the other night at your house?" I asked.

Diego blushed slightly. "Guilty," he said. "We were auditioning for Santiago's fortieth birthday party. Was it too loud?"

"Heavens, no!" I said. "I loved it. Any time."

"We were trying to mix perfect margaritas," Diego explained, "but we kept adding too much tequila—"

"And not enough lime, unless one lime is enough for a pitcher," Santiago concluded.

"Now that we know you, we'll call and remind you for the birthday party," Diego said. We said our good-byes and he and Santiago began walking away toward their home, the White Palace, a magnificent white

Moorish villa near my *casita*. But before they turned the corner, we were boldly confronted by a very tall, very thin person with a lot of wild black hair. I assumed it was someone I had missed at the meeting with Padre Juan, but I didn't know the gender, not that it mattered. However, while I was wondering, she loudly introduced herself as Madame Natalia of the Villa Viuda Negra. Her hands were as wrinkled as parchment and her bright white face, covered with rice powder, was framed by wildly flying black hair. Magenta lipstick wandered over her lips and the shadow of a mustache crouched on her upper lip. She wore a black cape to her ankles and on her feet were black plastic beach sandals.

"I have met these young men," she said, barely glancing at Diego and Santiago. "But tell me, my dear,"—she swung her long neck to face to me—"who are you?" Her voice was a throaty growl as her pinpoint black eyes settled on me.

I told her I was a writer, new to Paraiso.

"You're new. I didn't think I had seen you before." She looked me up and down. "I am Natalia," she said grandly. "You must come see me, come to my villa. Tomorrow at sundown for cocktails. Anyone can tell you where it is."

She fluttered away like a giant black moth. I watched her go. "Is she real?" I asked the guys.

"As far as we know she is real," Santiago laughed. "But be careful at her house. You never know what sort of cocktail she and her boys are mixing. Once when I was there they were reading a recipe from a book of poisons!" Santiago continued. "I suddenly realized I wasn't at all thirsty...or hungry."

"She seems like a nice old gal," Diego put in "as long as you don't get too close. She tends to be a little possessive. Let us know how the evening goes. And enjoy your cocktails!" Their laughter floated behind them in the sunshine as they departed in the direction of their house.

* * *

Cocktails, Anyone?

My town is not a typical Mexican village. The mild weather attracts people looking for a perfect climate and a good time, and they find it here—artists and heiresses, dictators and deadbeats, Nobel laureates and classical guitarists—all find what they're looking for in Paraiso. Even a Mafia bag-man and a crowned head of Europe found contentment here. Not necessarily together. Not necessarily *not* together, either.

The Villa Viuda Negra was a famous mansion and it stood alone at the end of a cobblestone lane in the historic area of Paraiso. Twisted trees arched overhead, and a single flickering gas lamp illuminated a massive mahogany door with a brass plate that bore the name of the property, Villa Viuda Negra.

I wasn't completely familiar with Paraiso and black night had fallen, so I had called a taxi to take me to the villa. On the ride from my house, the cab driver told me that the mansion had once belonged to a beautiful black woman, the most beautiful woman in Mexico and the favorite courtesan of the Spanish viceroys. Important officials used to come by closed carriage over a primitive road through swamps and forests to spend an hour with her, whispering secrets, making love, sometimes joining a gorgeous golden-skinned Spanish woman who was the black woman's lover.

But at the age of twenty-three, the legendary courtesan was murdered, stabbed through the heart with a single thrust of a knife on a windy, moonless night. Servants heard a cry and the clatter of horses' hooves vanishing into the stillness—a sound, my cab driver said, neighbors could still hear on moonless nights. The golden-skinned woman disappeared that same night, and the Black Widow's killer was never found.

The taxi stopped. I looked at a tiny sliver of new moon through the trees and asked the driver to wait for me. If I didn't show up in two hours, he was to come looking. He promised to wait.

I knocked on the door as he parked his taxi behind an old dust-covered Cadillac limousine. Its uniformed driver seemed to be asleep or dead, his head facedown on the steering wheel. A minute after I dropped the heavy door knocker, a maid in a black uniform and starched white apron opened the door and led me across worn Oriental rugs through an enormous, high-ceilinged salon, where brocade pillows filled every chair and sofa and gold-framed photos covered a dozen gilt tables. Books were stacked everywhere—on the floor, on tables, crowding an array of gleaming brass candelabra on a marble mantel above the fireplace. I glimpsed some of the bindings as I was hurried along—Freud, Jung, Erica Jong, The Kinsey Report, Human Sexuality, Bisexuality, *The Book of Poisons*. I followed the maid down a narrow flight of stairs to a tiled terrace where rattan furniture was scattered around an oval swimming pool. The lights were on. No one was there. The maid left.

I sat on a damp canvas deck chair and waited. Nothing stirred the water in the Venetian-tiled pool. There were no signs of Natalia, no other guests, no tray of clean glasses, no ice bucket, not even a potato chip. I didn't see a bartender, and the maid who let me in had disappeared. A small bar with three rattan stools and a half dozen liquor bottles stood at the far side of the pool and I walked over to investigate. I found a glass that was mostly clean and a tequila bottle that was mostly full, so I took them and sat down at the bar. I was pouring myself a tequila when I heard voices from a hallway. Two Mexican men, twenty-somethings dressed in white slacks, white polo shirts, and blue blazers, appeared and said they were Natalia's companions. One of them began mixing drinks at the bar.

"She'll be along soon, but we don't have to wait for her," he said. He and his companion raised their glasses with the Mexican toast to health, "*Salud!*" I joined them. We sipped in silence, smiling and nodding at each other with nothing to say. I don't know what they were thinking. I was wondering what the hell I was doing there and how soon I could leave.

Our hostess suddenly arrived, squalling and shouting like an angry child as she thrashed in the arms of a tall, pear-shaped man in a dripping wet terry cloth robe. Natalia wildly writhed and wiggled as she and pear-shape bore down upon us. Her hair was flying at the sides of her head and she wore witch's garb, with layers of long black skirts and a black silk blouse that had sleeves ballooning around her spindly arms. A joint was stuck between her lips, and she waved her arms as though propelling herself through the air while she kicked her feet and shouted in a gravelly voice as pear-shape tried to fit her onto a poolside chaise.

"Drinks for everyone right now! Where is that damned butler? I'll kill him! Someone find the butler!" she barked. One of the young men slid off his stool. "No, fix drinks now!" she commanded. He ducked behind the bar and grabbed two more glasses. I thought later I should have sneaked away when I had the chance.

The party began. I was fascinated, watching and listening as though my life depended on it. The pear-shaped man was Natalia's brother, Stanley, who lived in Toronto and was in Mexico on business. It was his old limo and driver parked at the door, where they had been for a week. The brother couldn't swim, and he was drinking rum and smoking a lot of marijuana and repeatedly falling into the pool in his clothes and thrashing his way to the side.

"Every time he puts on his suit and gets ready to leave, he falls in the pool and has to wait for his clothes to dry," one of Natalia's young men said excitedly. "He's been doing that all week! We're having a fabulous house party!"

Natalia rose up on an elbow and beckoned me to a white chaise next to her. "And what do you do, dear, besides blink those big brown eyes? Are you married?" She paused to inhale. "Living with someone?" Her bony hands fluttered to the neck of her blouse where her fingers rubbed the silk. "What do you like? Dirty dancing? Porno flicks? Midnight swim? Whatever it is, we can do it here tonight. They're darling boys, aren't they? We're having a marvelous time! Or, maybe you like me?" She thrust a hand inside her blouse and I feared she was going to show me some kind of body exhibition, but she only withdrew another joint. "Will you join me? It's divine."

The men were smoking at the bar, laughing frequently but keeping their voices low. The two dressed alike were obviously a couple, but who was I supposed to be? Natalia's entertainment? The brother's? If we were playing "get the guest," no one had told me.

Natalia's eyes darted over my face. "You'd like something stronger, wouldn't you, darling? We have whatever you wish. Hashish?"

How stoned would I have to be? I wondered. I shook my head and began to laugh. They all joined in, thinking I had said something funny, too numb to know that I hadn't said anything. Stanley slid off his stool and stumbled backward into the pool with a splash that sent waves lapping over the sides. "Oh, I've done it again!" he shouted, flailing at the water. Natalia staggered to her feet, spitting soggy marijuana, waving her arms and demanding that someone roll her a joint. I'd only been there an hour, but the party seemed to have peaked.

I stood up. "I'm sorry," I lied. "I must go. Thank you, Natalia." She looked at me, but she was past caring, close to nodding off. The two guys at the bar were in a giggling conversation, with a lot of groping going on. Stanley was hugging the side of the pool, staring at the water. His labored breathing sounded like a furnace. I took the stairs two at a time and went out the door.

"Calle Rufino Tamayo," I told my taxi driver.

"*Sí*, Señora." He started the motor. "And how was the Señora's evening at the house of the Viuda Negra?"

"*Bizarro!*" I said.

He turned around to look at me. "Too much party?" he asked with a knowing smile. He must have picked up other victims and survivors of the Widow's parties.

"Too much Black Widow," I said.

* * *

The Rich Are Different

I telephoned Santiago the next morning and told him I had survived the alleged cocktail party. "No cocktails, no guests, no food. Whose date was I supposed to be?"

He laughed.

I spent the rest of the morning working with Carlos, cleaning leaves out of the garden. I tried to teach him a few words in English but soon gave up; he was still trying to learn words in Spanish. After he left for school, I worked alone, listening to birds call, breathing deeply of the rich, black earth.

Around six o'clock in the evening, I heard a loud car horn honk. It wasn't a familiar horn and I ignored it until it sounded again. Irritated at having my quiet afternoon interrupted, I yanked open the gate and peered out. A Rolls-Royce was parked outside my house with Diego behind the wheel and Santiago sitting next to him. Both were pointing at me and laughing their heads off. I was speechless. The windows of the driver's and passenger's doors lowered silently.

"What now?" was all I could think to say.

"It just arrived!" Diego exclaimed. "We had it shipped from New York. Isn't it a beauty?" It was a beautiful car, but what made it rare were four unblemished tires in this land of retreads. The dust was settling when neighbors began gathering to stare. Noticing the crowd as he left Lupe's store, Padre Juan strolled across the street and nodded to Diego and Santiago. He gave the car a hard look and crossed himself. "Rich people in Paraiso?" he muttered. "Is it too good to be true? Please, God, let it be true." He crossed himself again and resumed walking.

From that day forward, Santiago and Diego were favored citizens of Paraiso. They charmed everyone with their smiles, constant thanks, and generous tips. Diego's approach to money was direct: "If money can't make my life run smoothly, what good is it?"

Despite Paraiso's simple origins, many people liked to visit here as though they were lords and ladies of a mythical manor, conducting their lives as befit the fancy places they had come from or dreamed about. Thus, Paraiso had its own social season, when banquets were celebrated in verdant gardens for jeweled women and men in tuxedos who danced until dawn. "The Season," as it was called, lasted from Christmas until Easter.

Santiago and Diego lived in New York most of the year, but at Christmastime they always moved into their palatial Moorish fantasy in Paraiso. It was a two-story mansion with six master suites and not a square corner in the place. Instead, it had minarets and attendant balconies—all swoops and curls—and enough Oriental rugs to carpet an airport. They called it the White Palace—Palacio Blanco. Set back and hidden in a dense grove of palms, it was all but invisible from my house, even though it was just around the corner. Their landscaping was a version of Spain's magnificent Alhambra, lush and shady, with the perfume of fruit trees and water rippling and dripping, cooling the air.

Uniformed servants hurried to unpack their valises and hang their clothes in large closets for spring's linen and tennis shoes. The minute Diego and Santiago arrived they began planning their big party of the season, this year celebrating Santiago's birthday. Because their permanent home was Paraiso, not New York, they spread their money throughout the village, beginning with a paint job on their mansion which employed a crew of a dozen men. Diego and Santiago had realized on their first day in Paraiso that it was much easier, and cheaper, to be generous and rich with Mexican pesos than with U.S. dollars.

Their houseguests luxuriated in villas which had been rented for them. The guests' needs were met by armies of maids, cooks, waiters, butlers, hairdressers, gardeners, laundresses, musicians, swimming-pool maintenance men, firewood vendors, and passing peddlers of fruit, flowers, brooms, vegetables, and no doubt marijuana—not to mention the electricians, plumbers, carpenters, plasterers, and painters who kept things running and shining.

As The Season gathered velocity, Santiago and Diego's jet-set friends converged to celebrate, their jets landing at Mexico City's airport or small planes navigating a strip of packed dirt and concrete near Paraiso, usually occupied by a ragged windsock and a farmer's wandering cows. Others took the train from Mexico City, making an adventurous party of the trip. Business boomed at Guadalupe's tiny store with sales of beer and aspirin, and at San Miguel church, where collection baskets were stuffed with dollars every week.

In those days leading up to his birthday, Santiago began drinking more alcohol than usual, his "usual" daily ration being a fifth of whiskey, one sip at a time. He confided to Diego that he feared alcohol was destroying his brain now that he was almost forty years old, but Diego laughed at him. It was just Santiago being dramatic.

One balmy night a circus came to town in two wheezing trucks and a barred trailer, hauling a bored-looking old tiger. A little yellow car had driven back and forth through Paraiso all day, announcing over a scratchy loudspeaker the arrival of the circus with a "wild tiger," "beautiful acrobats," and "clowns." Some of the houseguests, the first to arrive, decided to go without their hosts. They found their way to the circus tent in a field, bought their tickets, and quickly filled a section of the folding metal chairs facing the ring. They laughed themselves sick and loved the dinky show. As they watched, they hatched a plan for a birthday surprise for Santiago.

※ ※ ※

Green Man

The next night, a wealthy Canadian couple hosted a glittering black-tie dinner. Santiago was seated between the hostess and the artist, Lara Rivelli, well-known in Paraiso, New York, and Europe as a striking and smart blonde whose great-grandfather had been a Rothschild. Santiago was talking to Lara "very confidentially" of his fear of alcoholism when he fell silent to stare at something in the garden. He squinted his eyes, not sure what he was seeing.

"Excuse me, Lara, but do you see anything odd?" he asked.

It was a little man wearing a green suit, green boots, and a green hat with a feather. As he walked into view, he rang a silver bell and carried a glowing lantern.

"Well!" Santiago said loudly, when the leprechaun was gone. "What in hell was that?" A few people coughed, masking their laughter, but no one answered him. He looked at Lara with a half smile. "Was that a leprechaun, or am I completely nuts?"

"I'm sorry, darling, I didn't see anything." She covered his hand with her own long fingers. "Did you say 'leprechaun'?" She flashed her eyes at him and ran a hand through her hair.

Santiago smiled, expecting a joke. "You didn't see him?"

"No. I'm sorry. I would like to see a leprechaun one day, but I don't expect to see it in Mexico." She shrugged slightly as she raised her napkin to cover her smile. "Perhaps in Ireland."

He looked around the table. Everyone was staring at him. "Didn't anyone see him?" They shook their heads.

"Sorry," Diego murmured from across the table. "You've been hitting the sauce pretty hard. Why don't you not say any more about leprechauns?"

"But I saw him. He had a little bell—"

"You're making it worse." Diego frowned and Santiago fell silent.

The next night, the houseguests' party was at the spectacular estate of a man and his fourth wife who had abandoned Southern California for the "simple life" of Mexico. Their estate in the hills above Rancho Cortez included a pair of reflecting pools, a baronial banquet hall with a fireplace big enough to roast wild boar, fountains, an Olympic-size swimming pool, tennis courts, and a view of faraway city lights. Lanterns blazed in the banquet hall where tables fairly bowed beneath their loads of silver and crystal. Conversation was losing to a dozen mariachi musicians when Santiago leaped to his feet, banged a heavy silver dinner knife on the edge of his highball glass and pointed a finger: "There he is! See him?"

The music stopped while everyone looked where he pointed, but nobody mentioned the little man in green trudging through the hall and slipping out.

When the leprechaun appeared the next day at a luncheon in a beautiful restored hacienda, Santiago had enough. He was sure of what he was seeing, even though no one else seemed to notice the little man in green.

As soon as he and Diego returned home, Santiago said, "Something is seriously wrong with me. I saw the

GREEN MAN

leprechaun at that hacienda. This is something I happen to know about. I've read enough and heard enough to know there are no leprechauns at Mexican haciendas. Ghosts, maybe. Spirits, for sure. But leprechauns, never. I'm calling my shrink."

"I don't blame you for being worried," Diego said, looking away as he struggled to keep a straight face. Santiago called his doctor in New York. When he hung up, he said. "That's it. I'm flying up tomorrow. I'll be home by my birthday, unless he wants to lock me up." Diego didn't answer. As soon as Santiago left, Diego called a few friends and told them to spread the word that the leprechaun prank was over.

That night, as the leprechaun began his walk, Santiago covered his face. "Oh, no, not again," he moaned. When he raised his eyes, Diego stood and pointed at the leprechaun. "There he is!" he shouted. "Santiago's birthday leprechaun!" The guests cheered and laughed at the surprised expression on Santiago's face as the costumed circus dwarf bowed and rang the bell before he marched away.

For an instant, Santiago was frozen; then he began to laugh with delight at the elaborate prank. He raised his whisky and toasted his friends, surrounded by love and laughter.

Two nights later, the birthday party ended with a black-tie dinner-dance inaugurating the newest addition to Santiago and Diego's mansion, a domed ballroom. A fireworks show in the garden followed. When the fireworks ended, guests agreed they'd never seen such a spectacular show. There was a pause after the last starburst, then "FELIZ CUMPLEANOS SANTIAGO" burst into fire. To an appreciative round of applause, spent fireworks tumbled to earth as the partygoers made their way toward the sounds of dance music in the ballroom. No one noticed the glowing embers that were gently drifting onto the dry thatched roofs of neighbors' houses.

It was Padre Juan who called the fire truck.

He was walking through the neighborhood when he saw flames shooting out of a parishioner's small house. A pumper truck came from the state fire department, but it was almost out of water. Still, firemen struggled to extinguish the flames. Gardeners from every villa were roused from their beds to grab hoses and buckets. While firemen were shouting and tramping from house to house, oblivious merrymakers filled the new ballroom to dance the tango.

The next morning before dawn, neighborhood gardeners lined up at Santiago and Diego's front door. They had enjoyed the fireworks, they said, but wanted their burned thatched roofs to be replaced. They said there were fourteen. Diego paid for them all.

"I reroofed the whole damn neighborhood," he said. "They probably needed it, but just the same, I'm not shooting off any more fireworks."

※ ※ ※

Let There Be Light

The light bulb outside Guadalupe's *tienda* was mysteriously broken the following weekend, leaving her *tienda,* part of the church, and my house in the dark. When no one stepped up to confess and buy a new bulb, I decided to do something about it as a way of paying my dues for the good life I enjoyed. I went to Don Angel and asked him how much a new streetlight and a decent metal light pole would cost, and how soon they could be installed and turned on.

"I can get you the streetlight, but it will not be cheap," he told me.

"How much?" I asked.

He narrowed his eyes, trying to guess how much I was good for. "I'll come to your house tomorrow at this time," he said, tipping his hat.

At seven o'clock the next evening, he knocked at my door. "I have the price. It will cost you *cien dolares* for the bulb and the pole. We can install them tomorrow."

I waited. "Is that your best price?"

He looked as though he was deep in thought. He squinted at me from beneath the brim of his hat.

"I was thinking of eighty dollars," I said.

He paused. "I cannot do it for that. I must pay my workers something." He kicked a rock with his boot, watched the rock roll along the sidewalk, and then said abruptly, "Ninety. You have the pesos?"

"Right here." I counted them out.

"*Perfecto,*" he said. We shook hands.

"*Mañana,*" he promised.

SUDDENLY, MEXICO!

At six o'clock the next morning, a half dozen laborers went to work behind my house. Tapping a chisel with a sledgehammer, two of them began breaking a hole in the sidewalk. The ringing chip-chip-chip of metal striking stone is the most common sound in Mexico. It is everywhere. If you start listening for it, you will never stop hearing it. Like sirens in New York, it is a sound that is always there.

By ten o'clock when the workers quit for breakfast, the hole was a cubic foot. A mound of dirt covering the sidewalk was sliding into the street.

Day laborers were among the poorest working people in Mexico. Most of them were young, malnourished, and uneducated. If they worked on your property, they were apt to end the day stripping to bathe with your hose. It wasn't a political comment; it was taking advantage of a rare chance to be clean.

Don Angel's digging crew sprawled on the sidewalk when they took a break, leaning against the back of my house while they smoked cheap cigarettes. They looked about fifteen years old and were growing older before my eyes, breaking concrete with tools that hadn't changed in thirty-five hundred years. The youngest, a straggly-haired kid with black holes for eyes, was the gofer, running errands for the others who kicked at his feet to trip him as he ran. He collected coins from each and ran to the *tienda*, returning to hand out bottles of Sidral soda pop. Next, he ran to buy tortillas and came back to squat on the sidewalk and separate a stack of them while inhaling their sweet doughy smell. He took a knife out of his ragged pants' pocket and opened a small can of jalapeño peppers, which he passed around with the tortillas to be combined for breakfast. The men gawked and snickered every time a female over the age of ten walked by. After they smoked another cigarette, they went back to work, leaving their trash.

The chipping resumed, only to pause two hours later for lunch, a meal that duplicated breakfast. By nightfall, when Don Angel arrived to pay his crew, the hole was almost finished. After carefully counting their money, the laborers left in a burst of honking laughter to drink beer at La Esperanza.

Only three of them showed up the next morning. They looked sick, with pale, drawn faces and bleary eyes, and they worked slowly without talking. The others never returned.

The light bulb, a big white globe, arrived the next afternoon. A noisy red truck turned on Calle Rufino Tamayo, roaring like a circus beast until its air brakes shrieked and died in a hiss and the driver stopped it two feet from the hole. Attached to the cab and stretching three car lengths was a flatbed bearing a shining steel lamp pole held in place by a steel chain as thick as a man's wrist. A cardboard carton casually thrown next to the pole held the globe. Two men in faded denim were the lamp installation crew.

The truck driver squeezed out his door, slammed it and walked away. We didn't see him again until much later, when the new light was turned on and he showed up with his arm around a pretty young woman in a green dress. Unwilling to miss any action, the cleaning woman from the church crossed the street carrying her bucket and mop. She leaned the mop against my house before she mumbled good day and folded her hands to turn her attention to the truck. The two denim men unhitched the chains holding the pole to the truck bed and one opened the cardboard carton and extracted an oversize bulb, which he placed on the truck bed.

When Don Angel arrived after his *siesta*, it was obvious that this was more than a simple streetlight installation. It was an "event," a work of drama. Passersby stopped and watched, fascinated. Don Angel's laborers clustered around him and the hole. They were all discussing the project—the depth of the excavation, the width, the height of the pole—and always deferring to Don Angel. He took off his hat and put it on again. He measured the width of the street with his eyes, squinting for exactness. His lips began moving. A respectful hush settled on the crowd: Don Angel was thinking.

As more spectators arrived, they held their breath while they watched; then, a quick movement by Don Angel jarred them into action. "Let's go, *cabrones*!" he yelled.

With that, he pulled a flexible metal tape from his shirt pocket, briefly consulted it, and tried to swing it around his head like a rodeo cowboy's lariat.

"Right now! Let's go!" he shouted again, and everyone rallied. The crowd was noisy, full of suggestions, while the workers grunted and sweated, lifting and twisting the pole into position. When at last it was in the excavation, a cry of relief broke the air. The gleaming pole fit perfectly; a few anxious seconds of balancing and it stood alone. Don Angel provided buckets of cement and the job was done. At that minute a cherry picker turned the corner, its open aerial basket shaking above the street. The driver's helper fetched the globe from the flatbed and was lifted in the basket to attach it to overhead electric cables.

"Bravo, Don Angel!" shouted a man on the street. Other spectators congratulated Don Angel as they said their good nights.

"Thank you!" added Padre Juan, as the light came on while he was feeding his dogs. Hearing the commotion, he peered out his door to give the new light his blessing; it was the brightest light he had ever seen in Paraiso.

"That heaven may be so splendent," Padre Juan marveled, before he slipped Lobo and Canelo an extra portion of their daily bread.

That night Lupe kept the *tienda* open late, and at eleven o'clock, after customers had gone and she had rolled down the shutter, she joined neighborhood boys kicking a soccer ball beneath the brightest light any of them had ever seen.

✳ ✳ ✳

Music Of The Street

My studio in the garden was out of sight of passersby, but it definitely was within shouting range of every peddler on the street. As soon as the sun warmed the morning air, the flower lady turned the corner and walked down my block with a sweet smile, wearing her usual gold-rimmed bifocals and a bright cotton dress, and carrying on her head a wicker basket which overflowed with fresh roses—pink, yellow, palest peach-colored, dark red, and dramatic multicolored Botticelli. Waves of fragrance swept in her wake as she cried, "*Flor-es! Flor-es!*" as clear and sweet as a silver bell.

The shoe repairman came along every couple of weeks, pushing a bicycle and shouting, "*Za-PA-tos?*" at the top of his lungs. Sometimes, a buyer of old wrought iron joined the chorus with, "*Fierro vi-E-jo!*"—the words wrenched out and running together as though he was in pain from a terrible toothache. A knife sharpener announced his presence by playing a tune reminiscent of Ravel's "Bolero" on a plastic flute, up and down the scale. A boy selling steamed bananas pedaled his bicycle-powered cooker which made loud screeching noises. The balloon man whistled a high, chirruping call while holding a bobbing cloud of balloons that threatened to carry him aloft.

The two bells in the church belfry clanged mournfully of the deaths among us and joyfully of the activities of the living. When they called people to Mass, they had a ding-dong, hurry-up, get-along beat. Christmas Eve and Easter Eve brought wildly exuberant bell ringing punctuated by homemade fireworks set off one at a time by a grizzled man missing a couple of fingers.

A friend from the U.S. named Bebe, who had lived here longer than I, came by my house for coffee one morning after leaving her older children at school. Roberto, who was four years old, came with his mother. I gave him a bottle of Sidral, apple-flavored soda, and he played with the straw while we sipped coffee.

At one point, a street peddler of asparagus passed by, pushing a noisy wooden-wheeled cart and distinctly shouting, "Tequila!"

I had heard the cry on other mornings and it always puzzled me. Why did the asparagus man say "tequila"? Did he also sell tequila?

I asked Bebe, but she couldn't explain it. "It's just what he says," she replied.

Roberto stopped blowing bubbles in his soda to look at us. "I know what he says."

We stared at him.

"He doesn't say 'tequila.' He says 'un kilo.' He sells asparagus by the kilo." He blew a cluster of bubbles.

One day, July 11, 1991, complete silence descended on Paraiso and the light went out. So gradually did the light fade that many people didn't notice a shadow creeping across the face of the sun, taking it away. The shadow was the moon bringing darkness by obscuring the sun's light during a rare total solar eclipse.

Don Angel's rooster raised its old beak skyward two times that day—at the regular dawn, and again after the sun had disappeared and returned. Birds nested in trees or huddled in their cages, their wings wrapped around themselves. Dogs curled for sleep. Tiny slivers of light shaped like the diminishing sun danced on tree leaves and in the shade beneath trees. Streetlights turned on in the dusk.

Motorists abandoned their cars, leaping out to kneel and pray in the streets. The day went black save for a narrow ring of light around the darkened sun. In that minute of deepest darkness, the planets moved. The sun began to reappear and the rooster crowed. Dogs awoke yawning and scratching. Birds fluttered from their roosts. Drivers found their cars. People went back to work or home. The sun came out. Life resumed.

* * *

Good News

Someone was pounding on my gate.

I recognized Padre Juan's deep voice calling my name and hurried to let him in. It was four o'clock in the afternoon, *siesta* time, when the sun was at its hottest and sane people were resting in the shade. I poured each of us a glass of lemonade and we carried them to the table on my terrace.

"I have come directly from Mexico City with the good news," he said, sitting down. "The fiesta will go ahead. The church has approved alcoholic beverages for 'medicinal purposes,' shall we say, but not for everyone to drown themselves in a drunken stupor. Moderation is the key. I'm sure you agree.

"As for Padre Julio Cesar, no one can order him to leave Paraiso," he continued, "but there are ways to encourage a priest to choose a different destiny. In Mexico City, I learned there soon may be another church in Paraiso. Some parishioners of San Miguel Arcangel are plotting to leave if Padre Julio Cesar stays much longer."

"What's he planning now?" I asked.

"He says he will not baptize any child whose parents are not members of San Miguel church, and that he will publicly post the amount of money each person puts in the collection basket every week, with their name."

"The guy has gone nuts," I blurted out.

"Maybe someone is giving him bad advice," Padre Juan said quietly. "Be patient and say your prayers. Maybe he has a reason for his strong attitudes. Something we don't know about. Keep praying and we will see how it works out."

It wasn't long until it all worked out.

* * *

Uninvited Guest

True to their word, Santiago and Diego invited me to dinner. The setting was their "old house," a precious, rambling antique with leaded glass windows and hand-carved beams that had been abandoned by its rich owner during the Mexican Revolution. It had been bought as a ruin and lovingly restored by Santiago's French grandfather, who passed it on to Santiago in his will.

We were six to dine by moonlight in a garden in the historic heart of Paraiso, surrounded by staghorn ferns, massive palms, and majestic hundred-year-old Indian laurels. A full moon illuminated the dining table fashioned from a single slab of mahogany which was set with silver candelabra and dinnerware.

I knew most of the group: Santiago and Diego, Padre Juan, and Lara Rivelli, our lovely Italian artist friend. I made five, which left a chair for one more. I was glad to see Lara again. She was full of laughter and quick to smile, one of those instantly likable women who are attractive to men, women, little children, and big dogs.

We had finished our drinks and been called to the table on the ancient bricked terrace when the doorbell rang and the butler escorted a tall, very thin blonde woman to join us. Her streaked hair was cut short and she wore black silk slacks and a long-sleeved black blouse with lots of gold jewelry. Santiago introduced her to us as Countess Simi. We all smiled and kissed her on the cheek.

I knew a princess of Italy who was a "real hoot," as they would have said in Oklahoma; outrageous and delightful, telling everyone that she had twenty-seven royal titles and four ex-husbands, but alas, no money. When she told me, I said, "Go to Dallas or Houston, put an ad in the newspaper. Sell your titles and live on the money. Texans *love* fancy European titles."

"Oh, honey," she gushed, "I tried that several lives ago, but the ads were in Palm Beach and still no takers. But thanks a lot for thinking of me. Maybe I'll try Texas." The last I heard from her, she was living in Europe with rich relatives and planning to write her autobiography and tell all, in order to make a lot of money from people who would pay to not be included in the book.

"That's called blackmail," I said.

She laughed, nodding her head. "I know."

But the royalty at the party that night was not funny. She seemed harassed when she arrived and stood apart from the rest of us, shifting her weight from one foot to the other, staring at the old house, digging cigarettes out of her evening bag and lighting one. I was on the other side of Diego, with Padre Juan next to him.

"Hello, darling," said Diego, when he escorted her to the table and held her chair.

"Hello, Diego," she said brusquely. She puffed on her Marlboro Red. "Who do I have to screw to get a Campari, no ice?"

He hailed a waiter and ordered for her.

When it arrived, the glass of Campari contained ice cubes.

"I said no ice," the countess frowned, as she stubbed out her cigarette in one of the cubes.

"I'm sorry, madam," the waiter murmured. The countess threw the ice cubes on the ground and swabbed the inside of her glass with a lace-trimmed handkerchief from her French purse.

"I'll get you another drink," Diego said sweetly.

"No, of course not," the countess snapped. "I want Campari, no ice," she repeated to the next waiter. She lit another cigarette. "I've noticed that the people here in Mexico move very slowly," she said. "I wonder why that is. Because of the heat? Or is it a cultural thing?" Her perfectly made Campari arrived. She grabbed the glass as she stubbed out her cigarette and whirled around at me. "I can't live in Mexico more than four weeks at a time. I just cannot. And that's a long time. Do you live here?"

"Yes, I do," I said, trying to sound pleasant and nonthreatening, the way I had heard you're supposed to talk to unbalanced people. "In fact—"

"I don't know how you stand it!" the countess declared, cutting me off.

I didn't have a clue what to say, so while she lit another cigarette, I turned to Diego and began babbling. In a few minutes, I was drawn back to the countess, fascinated by her bad manners.

She kept smoking through the pasta course, furiously twisting fettuccini around her fork. She dumped in a teaspoon of crushed red peppers, tasted the pasta and glared at her plate. "I make *very good* pasta at home," she said loudly. Her plate was half full, or half empty. "I can't eat it. It is dry," she said, looking away.

Diego rescued me. "Do you know about the ghost?"

"A ghost? No," I said.

Lara overheard and her eyes twinkled. "Maybe we'll see him tonight," she said.

We pulled our chairs closer and waited for Diego to begin. Even the countess settled down, or maybe she had dozed off. While our wine glasses were filled, Diego began the story.

"The ghost was in this house when my grandparents bought it, and they guessed, from his appearance, that he had been here a long, long time."

"You mean he looked...ah...deteriorated?" I asked. "Dead?"

"Oh, no," Diego said. "Anything but. He was a fine-looking gent, or should I say, is a fine-looking gentleman, formally dressed in a ruffled shirt, long brocade coat, black velvet breeches, and polished black boots. By his dress, Santiago and I guess he has been here since at least the 1800s. The house was built before then."

"Does he do anything, or is he just hanging around?" Padre Juan asked.

"He plays the piano quite well," Diego said. "His favorite composer is Chopin."

"And have you seen him anywhere else?" the padre wondered.

"We haven't," Diego said. "Only at the piano."

"That's how we discovered him," Santiago said, picking up the story. "One night we had been out late, and when we came in, we heard someone playing the piano. We couldn't remember if we had invited guests for the weekend."

Diego leaned forward, eager to take up the tale. "I said I would see who it was, so Santiago waited in the garden and I went up to the living room, and there sat a man in elegant formal garb, playing our piano. He was good-looking, obviously a nobleman. I thought afterward he had smiled at me, but no one else had seen it so it may have been wishful thinking on my part. He was so handsome. Coal black hair and a full black mustachio. He looked like Zapata with the burning black eyes. As I neared him, he stopped playing and disappeared." Diego paused. "That was it. The end of the concert."

"But he's still here," Santiago said.

"Oh, yes, we've all seen him," Diego said. "And besides playing the piano, he likes to flush the loos in the middle of the night, but we haven't actually seen that."

"A man of many talents," Padre Juan called out, causing a round of laughter.

Waiters filled bowls with oyster velouté topped by Beluga caviar and conversation paused as everyone inhaled the delicious aroma. In the pause, Diego's cook in her starched white uniform approached the table and stood beside our host's chair. A few strands of brown hair showed beneath her toque and she tried to hide them while she waited for Diego to turn to her. "Señor," she said softly, once she had his attention, "there is a small problem in the kitchen." She looked at the ground. "Could you please come with me?"

"Maybe it's the ghost," Diego said, laughing. He excused himself and followed her into the kitchen.

A small back door opened into the kitchen from an adjacent street, allowing delivery and service personnel direct access without having to pass through the house or garden. The cook paused beside this door, which was closed, as usual. Her assistants were occupied with preparing the dinner.

"What's the problem?" Diego asked, taking in the busy scene.

Without speaking, the cook turned the knob and eased the street door open until Diego saw "the problem": a man was impaled by a large knife on the outside of the street door. A bone handle protruded from his chest, and blood had oozed from the wound. The knife had gone clear through him and stuck him to the door while he was standing on the narrow sidewalk. His dead brown eyes stared with surprise.

Diego was eye level with the corpse and intently studied the face. "Oh, no," he said, glancing at the weapon. "That isn't one of my new butcher knives, is it?"

"No, Señor. *Gracias a Dios.* Do you know him?"

"No, I don't. Do you?"

"No, Señor. Never have we seen him. We hear a noise, a thump, and I ask who it is. Nobody answers. I open the door. We don't know him. We're busy. We close the door."

"You did the right thing," Diego smiled. "Thank you." His staff waited for orders.

"Let's close the door and let someone else find him. I'm having a dinner party. I don't have time to bother with a corpse, or the police."

After the cook and Diego pulled the door shut and locked it, he returned to his chair and apologized to his guests for his absence. He grasped his napkin, leaned forward and declared: "Let me begin by saying it was NOT the ghost, and we are NEVER surprised by anything that happens in this house."

The dinner party ended several hours after midnight with laughter, Cuban cigars, espresso coffee served with tiny cookies, and many glasses of cognac. Bottles of cognac, as it turned out.

✷ ✷ ✷

Married Priest, Or Not?

A few mornings later on my way home from the *tienda*, I noticed people gathering outside the church. It was eight o'clock on Wednesday, an odd time for Mass. I started across the street, but before I reached the churchyard strong words flew to me from a growing crowd: "scandalous" and "intolerable," and the worst, "*sin verguenza*"—shameless. I hurried the rest of the way.

Word was flying through the village that Padre Julio Cesar was secretly married! It seemed that his housekeeper, a quiet woman with a pretty round face and soft footsteps, had become his legal wife. True, he was against the fiesta, and he was unpopular with his new moral rules, but married? Most parishioners were in an uproar. A few calmer souls, hanging back on the fringes of the crowd, wondered why the priest didn't continue living with her and keep the curtains closed.

Someone pitched a small rock at the church's double doors, a halfhearted toss, as though the pitcher had a change of mind halfway through the windup, but the small sound it made echoed in the church and was enough to send the aged sacristan, fearful in the shadows, hurrying to inform Padre Juan, who was attending to patients in the free clinic. Padre Juan told him not to worry, he would see about it. But the sacristan, in a state of panic, did the unthinkable. He called the police.

When a patrol car arrived twenty minutes later, everyone feared the worst. The nervous intake of breath sucked half the air out of the churchyard. The crowd by then had picked up a couple of balloon salesmen, a vendor of steamed bananas and ice cream bars, and three adolescent girls in dresses emblazoned with "Coca-Cola" who were handing out small plastic cups of Coke. The police were pudgy teenagers in wrinkled blue uniforms and scuffed black shoes. Afraid of the crowd, they scowled at everyone and shoved people out of the way with their nightsticks. They stopped in front of the closed church while one pounded his stick against a door. It opened and they sauntered through before it banged shut behind them.

The crowd waited as time passed. Those drawn to the drama took on a festive air of a day off, a vacation. They bought ice cream bars, Coca-Cola, balloons, and bananas for the babies. They passed the time exchanging jokes and gossip. No one was aware then, but Padre Juan had telephoned the bishop and they had spoken for ten minutes. He and the bishop got along well, but what was said remains private to this day.

Suddenly, the doors flew open and the crowd became still. The policemen walked out on either side of Padre Julio Cesar, protecting him from possible enemies, Padre Juan said later. Padre Julio Cesar gave a wave to the crowd before he squeezed into the backseat of the police car. The driver and his partner slid into the front seat and slammed the doors. The motor refused to start at first, much to the crowd's amusement, but finally it did and the car chugged away.

Was he married? Was it true or a rumor? No one knew except Padre Juan and the bishop—and Padre Julio Cesar, of course—but they weren't talking. Some villagers said he had been removed because he was too heavy-handed. Others thought he'd been removed because he was too married. In the end, the truth didn't matter. Enough people thought he was married. Padre Julio Cesar had to go.

We later heard that he and his housekeeper were living in a village in Tabasco, far from the rumors and truths of Paraiso. The next time I saw Padre Juan, I commented to him, "It's too bad what happened. Mexico needs more priests." I expected a nod, some sign of agreement.

"Not married ones," he said, and stomped away.

✳ ✳ ✳

Birdbrains

I live close to Nature, sometimes *very* close. I have shared my trash can with a possum, my bathroom with a baby owl, my ceiling with racing lizards, the garden pool with swooping bats, and a sunny spot on the terrace with an iguana. There was a very large white rabbit which stayed long enough to be named Bun-Bun before it chewed its way through a wooden garage door and fled in the night. Three collies, an Irish setter, a colorful procession of calico cats, and countless unnamed parakeets and canaries have come and gone, but one morning I awoke to more than the usual barks, bird trills, and animal sounds.

From the top branches of my Tulipan tree, a newcomer was announcing its presence with strident yawps, bird-call equivalents of fingernails on a chalkboard. I couldn't see through the foliage until a violent rustling shook the leaves and three iridescent green parrots fluttered out. Each was about a foot long and had a dangerous-looking curved yellow beak and very bright eyes that seemed to blink hungrily at me. I didn't go any closer.

As they took off and cleared the shaking leaves, they suddenly accelerated and were gone. I guessed they had come from Guerrero, the state south of Paraiso that rolls up from Pacific beaches through miles of uninhabited jungle and mountains where nothing much thrives but parrots, marijuana, and rebellion.

Within a week, three pairs of the parrots were spending their nights perched among the big bright orange flowers of my Tulipan tree. Every morning, I heard them wake up chattering back and forth; sometimes, they conversed a few minutes in a lingo like duck quacks. Then they flew away. I don't know where they went but they were gone all day. I like to think they were making the rounds of bird peddlers, freeing captives.

A houseguest of Santiago's heard about the parrots and phoned me one day.

"I hear you have some parrots in your trees," he said.

"That's right. Three pair."

"Oh, good," he said. "What time are they there?"

I told him I thought they spent the night in the tree, flew away at dawn and returned at sundown. He could come see them and take pictures if he wished.

"If you can get the exact times for me, I'll be over," he said. I was about to remind him that parrots—lacking wristwatches—didn't keep exact times, when he gave a sly heh-heh-heh laugh and added, "I don't want to watch them. I want to trap them."

I was stunned. I never dreamed someone would want to capture them, not someone I knew. I had grown fond of the wild parrots in my life. "In that case, I don't see any birds right now. They probably flew away." I broke off the conversation.

"Hello? Hello?!" was the last thing he said. I'm sorry a parrot didn't hear him. It might have answered.

Around that time, I happened to see the neighborhood wild-bird seller, a skinny man with a gruff voice who made the rounds of Paraiso every three or four months. He limped along, his wizened face shaded by an old fedora. He always had four or five little bamboo birdcages stacked up for carrying and filled with whatever he had trapped: bluebirds, jays, cardinals, hummingbirds, orioles.

Lara had telephoned to tell me the birdman was in her neighborhood and that she planned to free all of the birds. "I can't bear to see how they are treated, so many in each tiny cage. I'm going to buy all of them today. Won't you come and help me, Kate?"

Of course I said I would be right over.

Lara's garden was the size of a village green. From the large dining terrace of her villa, it took in a greensward, bordered by a dozen massive magnolia trees, and ended at a swimming pool of Venetian tiles. The garden overlooked a meandering river and offered an unobstructed view of the twin volcanoes.

By the time I arrived at Lara's villa, she had bought all of the man's caged birds. I joined her in the garden where her head gardener was helping. She leaned over the cages, speaking in soothing tones to the quivering little birds. The gardener, a gentle man who knew her mind, opened the tiny doors of the five fragile cages. We sat on the fresh-smelling grass with the scent of the magnolias in the air and waited for the birds to fly away. Lara was so happy to be releasing them that it took a few minutes for her to realize the birds were not leaving. They were staying in their cages with the doors open.

The gardener spoke up. "Señora, they have been in cages too long. They cannot fly."

※ ※ ※

Fiesta

I had been living in Paraiso nearly a year when I was violently awakened one morning by skyrockets screaming overhead and thunderous explosions like bombs in the sky.

The annual fiesta of San Miguel Arcangel had begun!

Wildly clanging church bells followed the explosions lighting up the sky while the shiny notes of a brass band erupted into "Las Mañanitas," the Mexican birthday song. Paraiso's most important annual fiesta always began at five o'clock in the morning on September 29, and before anyone could go back to sleep, or even think such a thought, steadily tolling twin bells, their ropes tugged by two strong boys, called them to a Mass.

Clouds of gunpowder mixed with incense billowed around the rockets, and the band played Sousa marches as it strolled and tootled through the crowded streets, followed by neighbors carrying candles and the costumed statue of San Miguel, temporarily taking a break from his church.

Near the end of the procession came Chinelo dancers, the stars of the festivities, wearing bearded masks and long velvet robes, their high, fringed headdresses topped with bobbing ostrich plumes. Maybe Padre Julio Cesar's threat to ban them had had an effect, because even though he was gone, no one misbehaved *that* badly as the Chinelos danced their jivey, jiggling two-step with a jerky rhythm that sent them spinning in circles. The dance traced its roots to wars between the Christians and

Moors, Don Angel told me. That made as much sense as any other explanation. The dancers and musicians were in perpetual motion all day and half the night, until one by one they fell where they had stood, in sozzled heaps beside the church.

People stayed as long as they could at the fiesta. As soon as twilight came, families began arriving in a constant stirring of dust and happy voices calling, laughing, swearing, joking, and singing. Mechanical kiddie rides and games of no-chance filled the narrow street in front of the church beside wooden stands selling tacos sizzling in grease, sweet-smelling roasted ears of corn, pink cotton candy, Cokes, and bottles of almost-cold beer.

After dark, screaming children were pursued by the "torito," a papier-mâché hood painted to resemble the front of a bull and shooting out fireworks, which was slipped over the head of a teenage boy who ran at the crowds to scare everyone—mostly little kids.

My neighbors' daughter, Blanca, had been chosen to be in the Parade of Floats the next day and her family and friends were thrilled. Alma and Don Angel, and their children, Blanca, Angelito, and Carlos, had worked for a week cleaning and decorating a flatbed truck which would be the float. It was scrubbed, painted, and adorned with palm fronds and silver tinsel. Alma had made Blanca a pink taffeta dress to wear for the parade and bought her new black patent leather shoes.

On the day of the parade, Blanca and five friends, all of them twelve years old, stood on their float as it led the parade. They giggled and blushed and waved to people, and smiled as though they would never stop smiling.

People in Paraiso knew this was the biggest moment of the children's lives, the day of large dreams. They were leading the parade! But most of the grown-ups knew that it would end too soon. Some of the girls would not complete seventh grade. Some would drop out of school to have babies. Others would go to work to help their families. Maybe one would attend a beauty school, and complete the course and bring home a diploma. The slow ride through the streets of Paraiso on a decorated flatbed truck was, for most of them, as good as their lives would get.

The fiesta ended one week later. On the last night, couples danced in the streets around the church to recorded music amplified throughout the village, and a thirty-foot-tall *castillo* ignited bursts of colors, one after another, to leave a magical glow in the sky.

* * *

And Another Fiesta...

Although the fiesta of San Miguel was the church's biggest annual celebration, it wasn't the only one. Because of Paraiso's rural roots, the people of the village always celebrated San Isidro Labrador, a livestock saint, on his day, May 15. A neighborhood procession began with the tolling bells of the church and the priest leading children dressed in their Sunday best, followed by a group of Chinelo dancers, and then the men of the church carrying aloft a painted wooden statue of San Isidro on a platform covered with fresh, fragrant calla lilies. Next came the band, its dozen musicians strolling along, and lastly, men and women on horseback or walking, some of the women riding sidesaddle in long skirts, and teams of oxen, scrubbed clean and adorned with colored satin ribbons.

The procession left the church, picking up spectators who joined along the way, and everyone walked a mile to a pasture which had been given to the village after the 1910 Mexican Revolution. It was an ordinary piece of land, about two acres, located in modern times above the toll road to Acapulco and within sight of a luxurious country club.

With a backdrop of the club's well-watered eighteen-hole golf course, the priest and people offered to San Isidro the planting of a few grains of corn and a prayer that ample rain and sunshine would bring a good harvest. The sowing of the corn was symbolic, but real corn always came up. When the procession returned through the streets of Paraiso, the sky always clouded over, a strong wind rose and rain poured down for an hour. Then the sun came out again.

The rainy season never began until June.

* * *

Living With The Day Of The Dead

I had lived in Paraiso three years before Don Angel invited me to participate in the Day of the Dead with him and his family. I accepted in the interest of broadening my *foclorico* IQ and maybe finally understanding this most Mexican occasion, a celebration when families join together to share a meal and remember their dead.

Don't let anyone tell you that it is "just like Thanksgiving" in the U.S. There is a major difference. In Mexico, spirits of the dead partake of the feast.

On the Day of the Dead, loud voices and laughter rose from the walled cemetery of San Miguel Arcangel as I followed Don Angel and his family in the stream of people happily going the same place at the same easy pace. With the fervor which we tried to give to life, we were going to celebrate death.

"We all have two things in common which you must understand in your heart, in your soul," Don Angel said as we walked to the cemetery. "We are born. We die. Better to laugh at death, as we laugh at life, than to cry or mourn. True?"

He paused to shake hands with a policeman and clap him on the back before he resumed leading the way. Flower vendors clustered around the graveyard's open iron gates where metal wastebaskets brimmed with carnations, roses, daisies, and especially marigolds, the sacred flower of the dead.

"You can feel the spirits getting ready for their party," Alma said, reaching out her arms as though to embrace them. "I love this part best of all, when we reach the cemetery and we are happy, feeling our loved ones gathering near us."

We were joining the spirits of Don Angel's departed family members—his father, mother, and grandfather—who were interred here. I had no one buried in that cemetery, which was why Don Angel, always gallant, had included me. Other families were already making themselves comfortable on the burial ground, spreading blankets to sit on for the picnic and setting up folding chairs near relatives' graves.

We walked slowly with the crowd, following a short gravel path to the grave sites. Most visitors arrived as we did, on foot, although a few came in taxis and private cars. Don Angel and I walked ahead, followed by Alma and their children, all neatly dressed and with their hair combed for the annual visit with grandparents and great-grandfather. Blanca wore the pink dress she'd worn in the parade, to show it off to them.

My neighbors were simple people, shopkeepers and farmers, middle-class families with the smallest, youngest members carried in someone's arms and the oldest supported by a cane or a helping hand. I nodded to familiar faces—the tortilla maker, Guadalupe from her *tienda*, Rodrigo the mechanic. Every family was carrying straw baskets from the market which they had stuffed with candles, flowers, and the deceased's favorite food and drink.

We set to work smoothing loose dirt around the tombstones and arranging flowers on the graves before it was time for praying, picnicking, and reminiscing with the presumably returned spirits. While Don Angel and his sons greeted friends, I helped Alma spread a tablecloth on the ground and arrange plates with Don Angel's ancestors' favorite meal: chicken enchiladas with green sauce and bottles of cold beer. When he and his sons returned, we all sat on the edges of the tablecloth to share the lunch, with plates set for each of us, the living and the dead. The enchiladas were delicious; the beer, cold enough. As the favorite dessert, Alma had bought us each a little sugar skull with our name on it, a traditional show of contempt for death. When Don Angel, Alma, their children, and I had eaten, three plates of enchiladas and three bottles of beer remained where they had been placed, apparently untouched.

As we lingered through the day, more laughter than crying filled the air as stories were shared for the spirits. Don Angel told how proud he was to be Paraiso's mayor. Blanca described the thrill of being on the first float in the fiesta; her older brother, Angelito, told his grandparents and great-grandfather how he had proudly carried on the family tradition by wearing the "torito" in the fiesta; and his little brother, Carlos, my gardener, said he hoped to wear the "torito" next year. Alma spoke about a sudden storm when a bolt of lightning had almost taken the life of her favorite cousin and a white carpet of flowers had fallen out of a clear sky to comfort him as he awaited help.

Night fell quickly, like a door closed on a lighted room. Candles were dug out of market baskets to be lighted and placed on graves. The odor of melting wax mixed with the sweet smell of copal incense drifting on the air as a light wind rose.

I asked Alma, "Where does copal come from?"

She thought for a moment. "When the trees cry, it comes down."

If, at the end of our vigil, none of the departed spirits' favorite food appeared to have been consumed; if the enchiladas remained on their plates and the beer had turned warm in its bottles, there was a simple explanation: the spirits had eaten and drunk the "spirit" of the food and drink.

The cemetery glowed beneath a flickering halo cast by the candles. People were seen as shadows as they packed their belongings to return home. As we made our way out, Don Angel confided to me that in past years some families' visits, fueled by alcohol, had turned into drunken brawls among the headstones.

"People complained they weren't able to carry on decent conversations with their dead," he said somberly, "so the police banned alcoholic beverages in the cemeteries, and overnight stays were no longer permitted."

✴ ✴ ✴

"Discovering" Paraiso

Former neighbors who used to live in Paraiso liked to come back on Sundays for Mass at San Miguel and to relive the sweet innocent homeland of their memories. The flowering trees and tolling bells reminded them of a simpler time in their lives. Other neighbors found in Paraiso a "special flavor" which enriched their lives, making the sky seem bluer and the sunshine brighter than anywhere else. And always among us were our most humble neighbors, dwelling in a different reality, sleeping six to a room that was damp in the rainy season and hot in the summer, while their children dreamed of a paradise called "Disneylandia."

For centuries Paraiso had dirt streets, but in the 1970s, the government got around to paving most of them. Ever since that happened, I have thought of my friend Santiago's prophecy: "If they ever pave the last street in Paraiso, it will mean the end of life as we know it." He was right, even though the paving project seemed to take forever as half a dozen workers trudged with shovels behind a solitary asphalt-dripping truck and finally covered the dirt road in front of the church.

Except for hidden lanes that twisted through remnants of orchards and sugarcane plantations, tucked into corners around the walled estates, and the crumbling ruins of Maximilian of Hapsburg's *casa chica*, that was the end. Once the new pavement dried, we began to be discovered—in much the same way Christopher Columbus had "discovered" long-existing "lost" civilizations in the Americas which had been perfectly happy living where they were, "undiscovered" for years.

On one particularly bright day, we were swarmed by clipboard-toting young men who earnestly came door-to-door, advising us that our street numbers had been changed by state authorities. I was told that my house, which had been Number 207, had become Number 53.

"Why are you doing this?" I asked one of the bureaucrats-in-training.

"Because there is confusion," he responded.

"Not on this block," I said. "All of our numbers are in order—205, 207, 209, 211..."

He shrugged his shoulders, looked off in the distance and walked away.

We were given six months to change our house numbers. Those became two years before most of us had posted new ones.

Paraiso's next visitors were the sons and daughters of Mexico City rich—"juniors," they were called—rich kids who giddily arrived to be married before hundreds of their closest friends jammed into our sixteenth-century church. When San Miguel Arcangel was built, no one thought about yuppie weddings, so there was never room in the church for all of them. But love knows no obstacles, and on they came.

※ ※ ※

Veracruz

A dinky little train used to run between Mexico City and Cuernavaca, and from there passengers could continue on to Paraiso by taxi or private car. It left Mexico City through an urban confusion of tracks, streets, and viaducts, ducked behind a string of warehouses and slipped into open country where it looked like a toy, crossing farmers' fields under the enormous sky. It was always a surprise to see the train in the middle of the treeless plain, puffing smoke and looking rather sedate as it crossed fields of haystacks.

I had been told by Diego that Mexican passenger trains always carried a caboose full of soldiers to ward off bandit attacks, but I doubted it. There was one way to find out, so Santiago, Diego, and I hired a taxi to Mexico City where we took an overnight train to the port of Veracruz to see for ourselves.

The train was shined up and spotless, with attentive service in the dining car and a smooth ride. We arrived in Veracruz hungry for breakfast and headed straight for La Cafè de la Parroquia, a landmark known for rich coffee and hurrying waiters. I don't know how many years Veracruz had been on my mind, coming and going like a sea breeze with dry palms blowing.

Veracruz is always surprising. Hernan Cortes made his reputation here as the macho "El Conquistador," ordering his soldiers to proceed on foot to subdue—and seduce—pre-Hispanic America. Emperor Maximilian of Hapsburg and his wife Carlota came by boat from Europe, expecting adoring crowds to hail them as the new Mexican royalty. Doors were slammed in their faces.

After a breakfast of eggs Malagueña, croissants, and steaming coffee, we strolled the port, touring the church Cortes probably established and the menacing fortress of San Juan Ulùa. Little shops sold what they could. Smooth turtle shells as big as end tables and shark jaws full of ferocious teeth were the most spectacular offerings, shell necklaces the most plentiful. We watched fishermen bronzed by the sun bring in their catch, *huachinango* and *camarones*; they splashed in the warm water as they guided their little hand-painted boats to the dock.

The overall mood of Veracruz was soft and rhythmic, more Spain than Mexico, deliberate as a *danzon*. As the sun went down, we chose one of the small cafés that bordered the *zócalo* and feasted on fresh red snapper with squeezes of lime juice, homemade French fried potatoes, and glasses of cold beer. People at nearby tables were speaking Spanish, French, English, or Italian; a trio of Cubans, huddled over their black coffee and rum, were speaking their own Spanish, with its soft and seductive syllables rolling like the waves. We could have been on the coast of Spain, down near Benalmadena, or in Italy beyond Genoa. We ended the night dancing lovely dances with the Veracruzanos smoothly guiding partners around the *zócalo* dance floor.

The next day we devoted to sunning and swimming, first at Town Beach and later at Mocambo. We stopped by the *zócalo* for a last dance and bottle of beer before we returned to our hotel to pack for early departure the next morning.

Our sleek Pullman was not in sight when we arrived at the depot for the eight-thirty return to Mexico City, but we assumed that our first-class tickets promised deluxe service. We were wrong.

A conductor in a shiny blue uniform directed us to a faded old locomotive sitting silently on the track with a string of rust-streaked cars behind it. Our car was the second from the end, he said, so we walked the length of the train, dragging our bags through the morning jungle heat.

We boarded and pushed open the heavy door to our car. The heat hit us like an open furnace, and the car was so ugly, so tacky, so not what we had expected that we were reduced to loud laughter. A torn strip of yellow linoleum covered the wooden floor, and wood-slat passenger seats on either side of the aisle had hard, lumpy cushions which seemed to have been stuffed with cardboard boxes. Windows were in wooden frames; you could push them up to partially open, or down to partially close, but they never completely opened or closed. After we were under way, we discovered that the bathroom at the end of our car was "out of order." I exaggerated calling it a bathroom. It was scarcely a room, with no place for a bath, and its large window was naked of a shade.

Diego, Santiago, and I were the only passengers.

I suggested we move to the last car, which was surely the observation car, with snacks and cold drinks and air-conditioning. We tugged our bags down the aisle again and opened another heavy door. It was the last car on the train and was full of young soldiers in wrinkled, sweaty uniforms, hanging out of windows and sprawling in the seats and aisles. Some hugged old rifles.

I spied a trainman through a half-open window. "*Los soldados?*" I asked.

"*Bandidos,*" he growled.

He blew a whistle and the train lunged forward. Thick green jungle enclosed us as we picked up speed to thirty miles an hour and maintained it for the next fourteen hours. It was motion, not speed.

After riding an hour, we stopped at a tiny one-room station where we took turns jumping off the train to use the restroom. I looked at our surroundings: no road, no village, no people, no electricity, no toilet paper. When we jumped back on, a man came through our car dragging a metal bucket full of bottles of Corona beer and chunks of ice. Thirty minutes later, a pair of women in printed cotton dresses and white aprons sold us plates of boiled chicken and cold, old tortillas. They sat on the seat across the aisle to watch us eat.

At the next stop, two adolescent boys boarded and posed in front of us. One held a stuffed coiled rattlesnake and the other held a small cactus in a clay pot. The rattlesnake's mouth was open, making it more valuable than a common snake, I was told. The kid with the cactus kept waving it closer and closer to my face until I thought it was "buy or die" time. I escaped by bending over in my seat as though I were looking for something on the floor.

Next came a dignified gray-haired woman in a long black dress who passed a small bamboo vase of white orchids through the open window at our seats and offered a gold-colored orchid as a two-for-one deal. Soon after she left, a middle-aged man with a mustache wearing a white suit that was too big clomped down the aisle in white shoes and trapped us in our seats. He smiled, showing his square-shaped false teeth, and then he threw himself into a sales pitch for magic salts guaranteed to cure impotence, corns, migraine headaches, "ugly fungus," and arthritis. He would sell us a brown paper bag of salts for only ten pesos. "*Garantizado!*" he kept shouting, in case we also suffered from deafness. If the "ugly fungus" came back—or anything else, named or unnamed—he would happily refund our money. Two boys in cowboy shirts and overalls serenaded us after the next stop, winking and smiling while they sang "Cielito Lindo" at the top of their lungs.

Our train left the coastal plain and climbed to high ground, where the air was cool and the sun faded into a gray overcast sky. Immediately, we felt a chill and pulled on sweaters. Except for the conductor, we were the only people in the car. We were enjoying a few minutes of silence when our reverie was interrupted by a small woman in a sequined dress and high-heeled sandals, who trotted down the aisle and stopped in front of us. She smiled and nodded, then reached a hand into the top of her dress and began fumbling around. We didn't have any idea what she might have been looking for until she whipped out a harmonica and began to play—faster and faster, in and out, up and down the scale—with a crooked smile frozen on her face. I don't know if what she was playing had a name, but she was fast! By the time she finished and her smile thawed, we were exhausted.

"If there is a harmonica, there will be an accordion," Diego said, joking, but before we knew it, a very large man dragging a huge accordion lumbered up to us and we were trapped in our seats again. He played a lot of scales, or maybe it was just one scale over and over, then he dragged the instrument back up the aisle, plopped it in a seat, and sat down wheezing beside it.

We stopped again, but didn't see anyone else enter our car. The train started and we thought we were alone until Santiago spied a little girl with curly red hair standing at the far end of the car, peering at us. I thought she was afraid, but she came our way, mincing down the aisle with small, dainty steps until she reached our seats. She held up an embroidered white blouse to sell us, but when we shook our heads, she left it on a vacant seat and returned to the far end of the car.

She was carrying a cardboard box when she came back. The top was closed, but all of us heard scuffling noises of something alive inside. She raised the lid and four kittens lifted their heads.

At that moment, the conductor came down the aisle with three mugs of steaming Café de Olla for us. The little girl closed the box on her kittens and walked away.

We did not buy any kittens. We bought everything else. I sent a bag of miracle salts to a doctor in the States, who sent back word that he "smoked the whole bag and didn't feel a thing."

At ten o'clock, we entered the Mexico City railroad yards, sliding past old boxcars where railroad workers lived. The conductor hurried back to us, his black shoes slapping the floor as he pulled down wooden shutters to block the windows. "The boys throw rocks," he said. It was scarcely out of his mouth before the first rock clanged against the side of our car. The train squealed and stopped. We stepped off, blinking in the sudden lights of Buenavista Station.

※ ※ ※

Carlos

As Carlos grew older, he lost interest in working in my garden. The quick little boy who had introduced himself so grandly became a moody adolescent trying to grow a mustache. I was kneeling in a flower bed one day beside him, showing him how to work the soil, when a stereophonic blast of cowboy music almost knocked me backward.

"I wonder why anyone would play a radio so loud!" I shouted.

"It isn't a radio," he said. "It's a *consola*." He let a handful of dirt slide over his hand.

I began again. "I wonder whose *consola* that is."

"It's mine." He stood up. "I have to go home now."

We still had a slight rapport, but when I heard he had quit school, I had to tell him good-bye. He had always known attendance at school was his primary requirement and had completed the mandatory six grades, but when he tried to go on, he couldn't keep up. He asked me if he could enroll in a computer school. I financed it for a month but it was over his head. I had to let him go. He stopped speaking to me.

Don Angel and Alma were understanding, and grateful that I had employed their son as long as I had. Carlos resumed speaking to me about a year later. It was a mixed blessing. The first thing he said was, "Can you loan me one hundred pesos?" I did, of course. He said he would pay back ten pesos a week, and he paid off the loan in ten weeks.

I had never thought about the exclusivity of Mexican banks, but they are not meant for everyone. Banks in the United States were the same way for a long time. The daughter of the creator of Bank of America told me that her father had begun his working life selling produce in California. As a peddler and an immigrant, his dream was that someday men in humble jobs like his would have the same access to banks that men in suits did, and he made it happen. But in many ways, Mexican banks were only for the prosperous. So when Carlos asked me to lend him money, I knew other doors were closed. I had become his "banker."

I still saw Carlos in the neighborhood, doing odd jobs and helping his father or mother at the market. Meanwhile, I hired Arturo, a boy who was a year from senior high graduation. His father was an accountant and, unlike Carlos, Arturo had experienced the benefit of early years in a good school and junior high. He needed money to continue his education and become a teacher. The Mexican public education system made few allowances for students on the fringes, either brighter than the others or not as bright as the middle mass. Carlos had slipped through the cracks. Arturo succeeded. I was honored when Arturo dedicated his graduation thesis to his parents, his teachers, and to me.

※ ※ ※

Bell Ringers (1)

My doorbell was an old iron bell hanging in a corner of the garage where a previous owner had placed it. Its chain was looped over the wooden garage door so it could hang down outside. I kept the end of the chain high enough to discourage passing children from playing "ring and run," yet low enough for an adult to reach it. The sound it made was "clang! clang!" like an old streetcar.

The bell had come from a *demolición,* a scrap yard in a small triangular slice of Mexico City's grand Paseo de la Reforma, where priceless artistic and architectural details ripped from elegant old houses—no longer anyone's "home"—were unloaded from dump trucks. Mindlessly jumbled, one upon the other, were antique iron balconies, carved wooden doors and sculptured arches, hand-hewn ceiling beams, marble columns and mantels, stained glass windows, enormous mirrored ceilings, precious angels and seashells of plaster and wood, all sold by their weight. Wrought ironwork was twenty centavos a kilo, *un veinte,* as the big copper coins were called. Carved wooden pieces were cheaper.

The owner of the yard, a grizzled, bearded man in dirt-encrusted overalls, had won a fortune in the national lottery in the 1950s. With his winnings, he had bought this small piece of land and all the tequila he could drink. His granddaughter, a delicate child in a flowered dress, ran the demolition yard by the time I went there. Empty tequila bottles ringed the property like staves in a fence. A few months after I had filled my car with treasures, everything was gone: the yard, the empty tequila bottles, the old man, and the delicate granddaughter; all were swept away in Mexico's relentless tide of progress.

* * *

Bell Ringers (2)

One Sunday afternoon my bell rang, and I looked out the door to see a small, neatly dressed man. He informed me that the telephone company wanted to change my number.

"As soon as your number is changed," he said, "callers will be automatically informed of your new number." It sounded too easy, too practical to be true.

A month passed and I had the same old number, while every day the phone service was worse. Misdirected calls went out, wrong numbers came in. Some days, the phone didn't function at all, a mixed blessing. Like Alexander Graham Bell, my daily mood was determined by the performance of the telephone.

One morning, I realized that the only way to obtain service was to track down a telephone company truck, follow it until it stopped, and bribe the driver to come to my house.

Santiago and I drove to the telephone company garage and lurked outside its chain-link fencing to bribe the first repair crew that left. This worked for us that morning, but as soon as other customers began offering bribes, the demand and the price doubled. Cars lined up every morning, drivers honking horns and desperately waving wads of pesos and dollars like refugees trying to buy their way out of the country.

After weeks of suspense, the telephone company called to give me my new number and overnight, my telephone performed perfectly. I thought my worries were over. My first call was to invite Diego and Santiago to lunch. But instead of hearing their telephone ring, I heard loud, scratchy *ranchero* music and a female voice telling me a number to dial.

"Allo!" a man shouted. "Allo!" It was not Diego or Santiago.

I told him the number I was calling.

"*Aieee, Dios!*" the man wailed. "*Momentito!*" Away from the receiver, he shouted, "Lupita! Bring me the list of telephone numbers, the old ones and the new ones!"

I heard sheets of paper being shuffled and someone sobbing before a woman yelled, "*Valgame, Dios!*" and the man came back on the phone.

"Here is the new number for your friends," he said pleasantly. "Please write it down."

The line went dead.

* * *

Spook Show

Mexico has always been an international listening post, a tropical "spy heaven" with swaying palm trees and good rum. During the Cold War when Mexico hosted the Olympic Games, spies of the world congregated in such numbers they threatened to overwhelm the athletes. The Organization of American States officially shunned relations with communist Cuba, but Mexico continued its sunny flights to Havana. Spies in Paraiso were active well into the new century, commuting around the world on their diplomatic passports.

There was no such thing as a "retired" spy because they never completely quit what they did. Several came to Paraiso as houseguests and stayed—superficially, at least—the ideal guests: charming, well educated, attentive, expensively dressed, and widely traveled. But there were a couple of drawbacks: they usually drank much more whisky than everyone else, and then they talked very fast and loudly about people and places everyone else in the room had forgotten. They also may have killed someone somewhere, but as long as they didn't "off" anyone in my house, I didn't care.

No one came right out and said he was a spy (women were not yet permitted to share in the glamour). Our spies masqueraded as "international businessmen," or "consultants" to Washington think tanks or newsletters, using their old-boy contacts and ex-wives's money to follow the good life. Spy-wise, they were discreet, their smooth talk and Princeton backgrounds pointing them more toward dry martinis than bloody daggers as weapons of choice. And among the dozen or so who turned up in Paraiso, I never met a spy who wasn't rich.

I invited a spook to a big party I was giving at my house one year. Diego, Santiago, and I gave it, and among our guests was Terrell Shook, a spook who lived in the neighborhood and had made a pass at me one night in his garden.

January was suddenly balmy that year. Tropical trees and flowers burst into bloom on hillsides and along the river, painting a patchwork of lavender, yellow, pink, and white. Paraiso was full of visitors weary of leaden skies and the party brought them together.

I was standing at the end of my living room, near the terrace. Diego was with me, greeting guests, while Santiago circulated through the crowd. Terrell joined us near the open French doors. As he glanced over the merrymakers, he suddenly grabbed my arm.

"Who is that? Standing on the terrace in front of the bar." I followed his stare and saw Madame Duval and her husband, Claude, from the French Embassy in Mexico City. I told Terrell.

"I don't mean her," he said. "I mean that man in front of her, under the light, standing sideways to the bar. Who is he?" Sweat beaded Terrell's face and his hand shook, rattling the ice cubes in his glass.

"That's Charles Erenfeld," I said. "His wife's an heiress. They live in Venice and winter in Mexico." I had never seen Terrell so upset. "Would you like to be introduced?" I asked.

"No, no." He was staring so hard I thought Charles would feel the eyes and turn our way. "I knew him after

SPOOK SHOW

the war. World War Two. In Europe." I waited for more, but that was all. He wrapped his hand around his glass of whisky and, lurching slightly, started through the crowd.

I followed him. At the terrace, he drifted left into the light and I sidestepped right to hide behind a stone column. I heard Charles speaking in French to Claude Duval.

"Charles Erenfeld," Terrell said loudly, interrupting the others.

Charles turned and smiled politely. "I'm sorry. I'm afraid I don't recall your name." He extended his hand, but Terrell didn't shake it.

"That doesn't matter," Terrell said, stepping forward as Duval and his wife backed away. "It isn't the name you knew me by." He seemed to be waiting for Charles to recognize him. Someone coughed on the other side of the terrace and I noticed that everyone had become silent.

Charles let his hand drop. "I'm terribly sorry, but you have me at a disadvantage. I don't know you."

"Rome!" Terrell thundered. "After the war! You were there! I don't care what the official version said!"

Charles closed his eyes as though trying to remember something. "I very well could have been in Rome after the war," he said calmly. He opened his eyes. "I have family there, buried in the American Cemetery. But I must say, I do not remember meeting you. And I am sure I would remember had I met you."

Terrell took a step toward him. "After the war, I had to clean up the mess you made in Rome. We almost had another war because of you, playing all sides. You left us to take the blame. You cost us a lot. My boys still haven't forgotten. Neither have I."

A few people began talking in lowered voices. They knew that they could attend parties all season and never stumble upon such a juicy scene.

Charles made another attempt at innocence. "It's possible I was in Rome when you say. I have been there many times. I have ancestors buried in the American Cemetery. I know Rome very well. But I must insist, sir, I do not know what you are talking about." He turned and walked into the living room.

Terrell stepped to the bar, ordered another Scotch, gulped it, and pulled the handkerchief from his breast pocket to wipe his forehead and hands. Party noise surged. People were moving but no one spoke to Terrell. He gulped another Scotch and paused at the edge of the terrace.

"What was that all about?" I stood next to him, half smiling, expecting a joke, something light.

His face twisted into a mask of pain. He put down his glass without answering. "Dirty liar," he said. "I must leave. Thank you." He lowered his head and burrowed through the crowd.

I bumped into Charles Erenfeld and his wife a year later at a small New Year's Eve party and he told me they were on their last visit to Mexico. "We've done this for so many years, I think it's time for a change," he said. "We have bought a manor in England. I rather imagine winter there is like living in a Currier and Ives print." The thought brought a smile to his face.

As I started to walk away, he stopped me with a hand on my shoulder.

"By the way, do you ever see that chap I met last year, here at your house? The one who gave me such a hard time on your terrace. What did he say his name was?"

"Terrell Shook, but I don't think he said it to you."

Charles frowned. "You're right. I'm sure I never knew anyone by that name."

✧ ✧ ✧

Max

Max the hairdresser moved in across the street from me one morning and took over a cramped, low-ceilinged space he named Salon New York. Pink painted letters on the plate glass window identified it as "Operated by Maximo Estrada, *Estilista professional*." He was a skinny guy and six feet tall, in black jeans, a wrinkled T-shirt, and rubber flip-flops. He had small black eyes, and his crowning feature was his thick shock of bright yellow hair. His voice was masculine, deeper than I had expected from his slim build and feminine persona.

The first thing he told me when I met him was that he took female hormones, which had given him breasts beneath his T-shirt, and he wanted a sex change operation.

Everything in his salon looked dusty and tired under two sixty-watt light bulbs trying to illuminate the black walls. The cement floor was covered with a thin gray carpet, and waiting customers had a choice of a brown Naugahyde sofa, straight-backed wooden chairs in front of a mirror, or a pair of bulging, faded lime green overstuffed chairs. A tiny black-and-white television shared a wooden shelf with a can of hair spray and a carnival-prize ceramic dog that held a stick of burning incense in its mouth. On the opposite side of the room, a pair of vintage metal beauty-shop chairs with hood-like dryers were separated by a huge potted cactus.

I learned over time that habits ruled Max's life. The first was that he constantly burned incense, probably to cover the smell of marijuana. I don't know if he smoked the marijuana or kept it for friends, but the incense smell was always there, sticky and cloying, clogging customers' sinuses.

I had experienced a problem with marijuana not long before Christmas that year, when someone sent me a large brown paper sack full of the stuff and I couldn't get rid of it! I didn't want to smoke it. I'd had my fill in the sixties. It was called "weed" then by the hippies and beatniks and down-and-outers, but once it reached suburbia, it became known as "grass."

Marijuana was abundant in Mexico. *Mota*, the Mexicans called it, and for years it was smoked only by poor or uneducated people—day laborers, conscripted soldiers, people without a job or hope. Some of my neighbors grew it at home or soaked it in alcohol to use as a balm for their aches and pains. I had never tried a stronger "recreational" drug. A doctor I knew in the States had killed an elephant with a shot of LSD. That was warning enough for me.

As soon as my gift marijuana was delivered, I began wondering how to get rid of it. I couldn't give it back without hurting the donor's feelings. Mexicans are serious about gifts, generous to a fault but quickly hurt if they sense you reject their generosity. I tried flushing a small amount, but it took forever and I had other things to do that day. My next impulse was to take it to the neighborhood Dumpster and pitch it in, but I realized that would have been asking for trouble.

The Dumpster, being a recent addition to Paraiso, attracted a lot of attention. People who lived on the margin of existence collecting trash and castoffs of the less poor paid close attention to what went in and came out. There wasn't any way I could anonymously toss in a bag of marijuana. The Dumpster habitués would know which house it had come from. I was stumped by the dump, but I cheered up when I thought of the cemetery.

Narrow streets ran along two sides of the cemetery and there was no watchman, day or night. I could walk or drive there any night and throw my sack over the wall. The dead weren't known for being light sleepers. But there was a drawback: What if someone were out walking, or in the cemetery communing with the dear departed, when the bag full of *mota* came flying over the wall? What if someone saw me walking in the cemetery and thought I was a prowler, or a robber, and called the police?

My next idea was to mail the marijuana with no return address to someone I despised. Names began dancing in my head. I would take it to the post office on the *zócalo* and hope not to encounter anyone who knew me.

Most mornings, people from the U.S. joined other foreigners at sidewalk cafés near the post office to read their mail, drink coffee and chat. If I went with the sack of marijuana and saw someone I knew, I would avert my eyes and walk very quickly, but not so quickly that I looked suspicious; just at a normal quickly walking speed. Who would be the recipient of the marijuana? Too many names came to mind as the faces of inept individuals rolled by like credits at the end of a bad movie. I could never choose just one.

I forced my thoughts closer to home. I could bury the marijuana in my garden. That would be appropriate, because it grows everywhere. After the Paraiso penitentiary was closed, marijuana sprouted on all sides, even among the pastel-painted kiddie cars at the playground.

For me, burying it meant digging a hole in my garden on the gardener's day off and inventing a reason for the hole. Maybe I could plant a tree and fill the hole with my stash and dirt. But what if the marijuana killed the tree?

At a party I offered marijuana to friends, and they seemed excited and promised to come get it, but they didn't come. I couldn't even *give* it away! As a last resort, I decided to drive down the toll road to Acapulco and leave it on the roadside. I doubted I would be seen or recognized. But then I remembered that a few months earlier, on the same highway, a driver had stopped on the shoulder and thrown a dead body out of his trunk and nobody paused. I finally decided not to worry about it—a solution would come.

Max's other habit was to dress in his only long evening gown—green taffeta sleeveless with a low neck—and high heels and stroll the streets of Paraiso after he closed his shop for the day. Sometimes, guys from the police academy accompanied him, other times he was trailed by a crowd of giggling, skipping children.

For six months, he was famous as the star in a weekly drag show at a shabby discotheque near the big central market. The market was dark at night, and the disco was so dark you could hardly see your hand in front of your face—or anyone else's face, either—or their hands, which was no doubt the objective of the dim lighting. The place had weak drinks and a strong smell of rotting vegetables, but Max didn't complain. He was *La Estrella*, The Star, and when the spotlight was on him, screaming fans cheered while he had the "honor," as he called it, to lip-sync songs of Judy and Barbra and Marlene, strutting and swirling in his green taffeta as though there was no tomorrow.

Soon after Max moved in, I told a society lady from Mexico City about him. A few days later, I was in my kitchen when a long black car pulled up and I watched, fascinated, as my friend's chauffeur fairly slunk into Max's salon with armloads of gowns that glittered with pearls and sequins and beads. When he left an hour later, he was empty-handed. He got in the car and zoomed away.

Max emerged in a flash, his face glowing as he sang out, "Beautiful dresses for the star! Take a throne and I'll tell you what happened, darling," he said, motioning to one of the salon chairs.

"I took the gowns on consignment. The chauffeur said the Señora will let me wear them until I sell them. They all fit me perfectly. I like the Valentino best. He's so divine. The chauffeur thought I looked lovely in it,"—he paused a beat—"and what a man *he* is!"

Max carefully hung each gown on its own padded hanger. The display of elegance in the shabby salon was startling. Carolina Herrera was next to Dior, Versace next to Prada. In the center was the red Valentino. During the next month, Max wore a different gown every Saturday night, making his entrance to waves of applause. After the first Saturday, word of the beautiful gowns swept through Paraiso, and soon more women than men were in the audience, shouting, "Take it off!" and "Throw it here!"

He saved the Valentino for "special performances," private midnight affairs for politicos and millionaires. Paraiso had always been tolerant of artists and oddballs. "Learn to live with your neighbors" was the unwritten message. Benito Juarez, the great Mexican patriot, had written it: "Respect for the rights of others is peace."

Max had a mixed but loyal clientele. His mother wore her print rayon dress and rode the bus two hours from her village every Saturday to see her "boy" and have her hair washed. She was a country woman, simple and quiet. Sometimes, Max's young nieces and nephews visited, the girls preening before the mirrors while the little boys sat outside on the steps and pitched pebbles.

Only one neighbor openly disapproved of his behavior. He was a Mexico City entrepreneur whose weekend estate was near San Miguel church. Many times when Max was outside his salon talking or flirting, this man drove by with his chauffeur at the wheel. At first, he simply frowned, but then he began turning his head away. To him, Max's persona was definitely non grata. One night, as a group of us was leaving a restaurant near the salon, Max was out on the street in a yellow chiffon strapless number.

"I think that's disgusting," the entrepreneur said.

I said, "I think he enlivens Paraiso. It certainly isn't boring."

The entrepreneur looked at me. "As you Americans say, I'll have to think about that."

One day, Max came to tell me he was moving. Water had leaked into his shop and the owner didn't want to fix it. Max had found another place a few blocks away where he hoped to make more money. Then he was gone and his old salon was vacant. The entrepreneur asked me one day what had happened to Max and I told him he had moved.

"He did add spice," the man observed.

Max greeted me at the door the first time I went to his new salon. It was smaller than the old one, with a couple of new mirrors but the same brown sofa and overstuffed chairs. The trophy dresses were displayed on the new walls.

I was at my wit's end about the marijuana, so I asked Max if he wanted it.

"I can get rid of it for you," he said. "All things are possible. I'll give it to some cops I know and they'll either get credit for it as a 'seizure,' or they'll smoke it." He smiled and waved as I left, relieved.

The days turned into weeks. Every now and then, I thought about Max and the marijuana, but I kept putting off delivering it. Then someone told me he had been sick, uremic poisoning, and I went to see him and took the marijuana. He looked pale and thinner, but his smile was quick and he thanked me again for sending my friend's chauffeur with the gowns.

"I will never be able to buy them, but I love to wear them," he said. "They have made my life complete. I plan to wear all of them."

SUDDENLY, MEXICO!

Max was rare. Even as he faced his last long illness, he never lost his spirit or his enthusiasm for life. But he never had his sex change operation. Three months after moving into his new Salon New York, he died at home. His mother, nieces and nephews, and friends gathered around. He had said he wanted to be buried in the red Valentino. Padre Juan, ever faithful, agreed.

※ ※ ※

Knowing Helen

I met the actress Helen Hayes when I was asked by a friend to hang a beautiful silken swag of spring flowers above her bed in her Cuernavaca villa. I got the job because I was tall, and the gardener was tall, and he and I attached the swag over an antique angel which was the focal point of Miss Hayes's bedroom.

All went well in that room full of sunshine and flowers. The decorator, my friend Bebe, told me later that she was apprehensive that the angel would fall on the star's head and she would have to flee. That was a routine reflex for countless Mexican bus drivers in similarly dire circumstances, described by headlines as "Bus Crashes in Ravine, Driver Flees."

Little did I know that Helen was to be my own guardian angel for the next fifteen years while we wrote and fine-tuned her life story. Our shared reward was being on the New York Times Best Seller List, but my most precious reward was her friendship.

That day was the first time Bebe and I were invited to share luncheon in the garden of the most celebrated American actress in history. We realized that far from being aloof or standoffish, she was a kind and intelligent woman with a quick sense of humor and an appreciation for what life and love had given her.

She was born in 1900 in Washington, D.C., and began acting on the stage when she was five. After her first performance, she told her mother she didn't want to leave the theatre. She didn't leave until she retired in 1972, after her last role, as Mary Tyrone in Eugene O'Neill's masterful *Long Day's Journey Into Night*.

Since the 1950s, she had divided her time between her rambling house overlooking the Hudson River in Nyack, New York, and her Mexican Colonial villa in Cuernavaca on the street named for a poet-king, Netzahualcoyotl.

She happily adapted to a Mexican routine, hosting and attending leisurely garden luncheons, exploring old ruins, poking around the shops, working in her beloved garden, participating with Father William Wasson's international orphanage, and entertaining friends from far and near until she died in 1993 on St. Patrick's Day—the day on which she always proudly celebrated her Irish heritage.

Her kindly face with twinkling blue eyes was familiar to millions; her voice with its clear diction was unforgettable. Her posture was perfect. She wore her hair in a bun on the top of her head and loved to wear a manta or brightly colored Mexican dresses from the public market. She relished *agua de Jamaica*. When her friend, the early day actress Lillian Gish, visited Mexico, Lillian always called it "drinking flowers."

Bebe, a friend and decorator, helped Helen transform her Mexican Colonial home into a "Mexican grandmother's house" after three male decorators had insisted on making it into a "star's" home.

"I don't want that. I've had that," Helen had said. What she needed was someone to help her who shared her affection for Mexico, and for grandmothers.

Working with Helen's choices, Bebe brightened the living room with cushions covered in vivid Mexican colors. A delicately woven couch cover from India that drew together the bright colors of the room was mounted as a dramatic wall hanging. Upstairs, Miss Hayes's brass bed was given fine cotton and lace blanket covers embroidered with pastel-colored angels and "*Buenas Noches Mi Amor.*" Guest room beds received the same lovely treatment. As a final touch, she arranged the flowered swag over the bed, affixed to the wall above the brass headboard with the beautifully carved and painted antique angel's head.

It was at this time, 1978, that I decided to write a children's guide to the fun in Mexico. Helen had always loved Mexico, and perhaps thinking of her late daughter, Mary, who also had loved the country, she said she would like to participate in the book. We began composing *MEXICO FOR FUN*, but I felt Helen deserved her own space. I suggested that she write about what she knew best: her life in the American theatre. That was what the public wanted to read, I insisted.

A month later, she asked me, "If I agree to do the book you were talking about, how would we do it?"

I explained that we would work in Cuernavaca, and I could go to Nyack and work when she was there and had time. She agreed with a nod.

The day we began working, I arrived at Helen's house in Cuernavaca at the appointed time with my supplies in a satchel. I took out a pad and pen, started a tape recorder, and her story unrolled in her vibrant, inimitable voice for the next ten years.

One day when Bebe and I had stopped by her garden for a minute, a maid came to tell Miss Hayes she was wanted on the telephone.

"Get their name and tell them I'll call back." Helen said distractedly.

The maid left and came right back. "It's the *Casa Blanca*," she said.

"Oh," Helen said, standing up. "Excuse me a minute." She followed the maid to the house.

When she returned, she apologized for her absence and said, "It doesn't make any difference to me who the occupant is—when the operator says, 'White House calling,' it always gives me a thrill."

Bebe smiled. "When my telephone rings and the maid tells me it's la Señora Helen calling, it gives *me* a thrill."

On a sunny afternoon when Bebe and I visited Helen, we were preparing to leave when she said, "Could you please stay a little while longer? Gloria Swanson telephoned and she's coming over. I can't abide that woman. Would you mind awfully staying?" Wild horses couldn't have dragged us away. Gloria Swanson had been a silent film star and returned to the screen to cap her career with *Sunset Boulevard*, the sensational film directed by Billy Wilder.

Helen was wearing a white cotton manta dress with a turquoise necklace and turquoise shoes. Her hair was pulled up neatly on top of her head, but some escaped and trailed softly down the back of her neck. Gloria arrived in a swirl of blinding white—slacks and jacket, her hair in a white turban, a large white leather purse that was monogrammed. Her arms were adorned with wide gold bracelets, one of which was also monogrammed. I thought the enormous "GS" on her tiny arm must have been quite a burden. They greeted each other with faint smiles, cheek to cheek, kisses in the air.

"How have you been, Gloria? Would you like tea or something? Have you had lunch?"

"Oh, heaven's no. I'm on a very strict diet."

"Maybe some Jamaica water?"

"Oh, no, Helen. I can't drink anything like that."

Gloria opened her large white leather purse with the gold "GS" monogram and withdrew a small, sealed plastic bag. "This is all I eat," she said, holding up the bag for all to see. It contained thin slices of celery and carrots.

"Interesting," Helen said.

"I've been in New York. I feel terrible. I hate New York," Gloria said, carefully tucking the plastic bag back into her purse.

"Do you really? I love New York."

"I hate everything about it. I don't do well there, but I had to go. I love California."

"Oh."

"Don't you love California?" Gloria asked her.

"No, I don't. My son lives there and he seems to like it, but I love New York. I feel good when I'm there."

They volleyed for thirty minutes, these two stars who couldn't quit. If it had been a tennis match, they were at deuce when Gloria made her exit and Helen thanked us for staying and told us good-bye.

A couple of nights later, Helen's neighbor, Ray Cotè, gave a small dinner party for Gloria and featured a special chicken dish he had created for Villa Santa Monica, his famous hotel in Morelia, Mexico. Also invited were Helen and her houseguests, a honeymooning couple who had worked with her in the theatre. They were excited that they were going to dine with Gloria Swanson, and as a favor, the host had seated the young husband next to Gloria.

But while everyone entered the dining room, Gloria stood outside it, saying in a loud voice, "Don't eat the chicken! Do you know there is a cupful of pus in every chicken?"

"Gloria is carrying this diet business too far," Helen said the next day. "What she said, no one should ever say to another person. And to pull that in front of my sweet houseguests was too much."

Helen came to Mexico in 1943 during World War Two while her husband, the playwright Charles MacArthur, was serving in the military. Helen brought her daughter, Mary, to witness the birth of the volcano Paricutin in the state of Michoacan and they stopped in Cuernavaca, where Helen's brother-in-law and his wife had a winter residence. During their stay, everyone gave them advice on how to dress for their excursion. Any exposure of skin would be dangerous, they were told, so they went to the public market and bought pith helmets, railroad engineer's gloves, long socks, long-sleeved shirts, bandanas, and goggles. They drove to Uruapan, the closest town to the site, where the earth had started smoking in a farmer's cornfield.

The town was overflowing with people from around the world who had come to see this volcano being born. Many stayed awake all night, talking and singing in their native languages, too excited to sleep. Others slept in the streets, but Helen wisely had reserved a room in a small hotel. The next morning, she and Mary dressed, carefully covering their skin. When their guide came, he looked at them and burst out laughing.

"We looked like beekeepers," Helen said.

They set off cross-country in a rattletrap car, passing near a village where molten lava flowed. As they began to ascend, they were instantly engulfed in an all-black landscape. Everything was buried under a fine lava dust except a church steeple—all that remained of a village. They exchanged the car for horses and rode toward the crater. They could hear the volcano's thunderous roar before they saw it. The air was full of smoke and huge boulders that were being hurled out to come crashing down around them. People watching said the boulders were as big as Chryslers, Helen recalled.

A Mexican boy watching them befriended Mary and showed her how to use a rock in each hand to hold a chunk of glowing lava. The boy and Mary ran up the side of the volcano, which gave Helen a fright until they turned around and came back laughing.

As they were about to leave, Helen heard an American woman's voice with a loud twang say, "Are you girls about ready to go and eat now?"

She whirled around and saw three middle-aged American women in short-sleeved cotton dresses and comfortable shoes. No gloves, no pith helmets, no long sleeves or pants or bandanas. They were wearing what they wore every day and no little volcano was going to make them change their habits.

Before Xochicalco appeared in travel guides, Helen and John Richards, a good friend and neighbor, ventured there in style. John packed a picnic hamper, stowed a couple of bottles of wine, and they set off in his elegant Rolls-Royce to take rubbings at what was then an abandoned temple in the countryside twenty miles south of Cuernavaca.

A "rubbing" was an impression of a bas relief obtained by placing a piece of cloth or paper over the sculptured surface and rubbing it with graphite or daubing it gently with paint. It was an ancient custom which became popular again in the 1950s when Helen and John made their trip. Helen provided the rubbing materials: manta cloth, lamp black, and sponges to apply the lamp black to the cloth.

Xochicalco was mostly a ruin devoid of roads or pathways, a tangle of small trees and scratchy grasses, barely excavated. Local people took target practice there, lining empty bottles along the edges of ancient pyramids to shoot at them. One beautiful stone section dedicated to the sacred Plumed Serpent had been uncovered, and it was this that Helen and John wanted to capture.

They parked near the dirt-covered complex and quickly found the Plumed Serpent. The only sounds were birds and insect noises under the lazy sun as they set up their materials. Helen went first, daubing lamp black with a sponge over the white manta they had taped to the pyramid's face. The impression was barely visible.

"Try again," John said.

Helen pressed harder on the cloth, but the next impression was no better.

John had another idea, and he removed a sack from the car. "How about this?" he asked, pulling out a paint roller and a can of gooey black enamel.

"Oh, my, I don't know," Helen said.

"Let's try," he said, and he opened the can of paint and dripped it onto the roller. "You first, Helen."

She taped a new piece of manta to the carving and, at John's urging, pushed the paint roller up and down on it. She raised a corner of the cloth to see her work. The sculpture was completely covered in thick black paint. It had soaked through the cloth.

Her reaction was immediate: "I was over fifty, but I raised my skirt and ran like a gazelle. I ran and hid in the car." A minute later John joined her and they slammed the doors. "I don't know how we expected to hide in a Rolls-Royce in the middle of nowhere," Helen recounted, "but I knew I had ruined the sculpture and I was afraid someone would find it and come after me."

She was so afraid that she didn't return to Xochicalco for ten years. When she did go back, she saw with relief that the sun and rain had cleansed the Plumed Serpent of all traces of black.

※ ※ ※

Bulls

When Helen heard about a Pamplona-style "Running of the Bulls" planned for the town of San Miguel de Allende in 1973, she telephoned and invited Bebe and me to accompany her. It was a few hours' drive from Cuernavaca and we had a friend there who owned a large apartment above El Jardin. The apartment, from which we could watch the festivities, had a wide balcony almost a block long upstairs above the sidewalk. Beneath it were the open doors of El Colibri bookstore and a shop selling glassware.

We drove to San Miguel on Friday. Helen had a hotel room and Bebe and I stayed with our friends. It rained Friday night. We had planned to walk to a popular restaurant but drizzle kept falling. Fearing the worst with our famous guest—the paving stones were as slick as ice—we took our car, drove four blocks and collected Helen at her hotel, drove three blocks to the restaurant, let her out and parked.

The next morning, we collected Helen in a taxi and rejoined our friend at her apartment. We had the entire balcony to ourselves from which to watch the "Pamplonada" safely above the crowds.

The black bulls arrived in El Jardin stuffed into a truck with high wooden sides. They were smaller than I had imagined, and rather timid. In the absence of barricades to protect the spectators from the bulls, and vice versa, everyone was simply turned loose—bulls and people—to begin trotting around El Jardin.

SUDDENLY, MEXICO!

Some bulls went the wrong direction. Some sat down. Some seemed to be looking for the truck, or their mother. The noisy crowd ran with them and away from them, waving their arms and occasionally falling down. Some bulls made halfhearted attempts to push the people out of their way. We ran back and forth on our balcony, watching the show. Every now and then, someone walking in the street looked up and, recognizing Helen Hayes, would wave and shout greetings, to which she always responded with a big wave and a smile.

Suddenly, we heard a terrific commotion beneath us, the noise of things being broken: glasses, windows, furniture. We thought it was a fight—a lot of drinking was going on—and we hurried to the front of the balcony, leaned over as far as we dared and looked below. When Helen saw what was causing the racket, she began to laugh.

"For the first time in my life, I've seen a real bull in a china shop!" she exclaimed. We all stared as a slobbering black bull slowly emerged from the wreckage of the glassware shop beneath us. It glanced up at our hanging-upside-down faces and casually trotted away.

St. Patrick's Day was always the occasion for a special fiesta by Helen because her beloved grandmother, Graddy Hayes, was Irish. Helen invited forty people for four tables of ten around the sparkling antique fountain on her terrace. We made sure that our green clothes were ready for the day, and then we all hoped that we were among the chosen.

Each year, Helen had Irish favors at every plate, and the menu at her luncheon was corned beef and cabbage, Irish whisky, and Irish coffee. There was always a program. One year, Helen and Maurice Evans, the acclaimed Shakespearean actor, recited scenes from Shakespeare that brought tears to her guests' eyes. On another delightful St. Patrick's Day, they declaimed favorite love poems. To be on Helen Hayes's antique brick terrace with the sun shining in a flawless sky and birds singing in the garden, to hear her voice and the deep, dramatic voice of Maurice Evans speaking the timeless words of William Shakespeare, was to know how glorious life could be.

One year we heard the chorus from Father Wasson's children's home; another year, Helen asked me to tell about the San Patricio Battalion, Irish immigrants who deserted the U.S. Army to fight on the Mexican side in the war of 1846–1847—called an "invasion" in Mexico—which ended with Mexico losing half of its territory. This became the states of Texas, Arizona, New Mexico, Nevada, California, and parts of Colorado and Wyoming—all sold to the United States for a total of fifteen million dollars.

Nearly ten years passed before the book with Helen was completed. On the last day, Helen and I were sitting where we had begun, upstairs in her sunny bedroom in Cuernavaca. "Well, that's it," Helen said, as she read the last page. "What do we do now?"

I had brought a chilled split of champagne and glasses in my purse. I withdrew them now, popped the cork, and we toasted to the success of the book.

"There is one more question I have," I said.

"Something you've saved until the last in case I got mad and ruined the book," she said.

"That's pretty much it," I confessed. "I have heard from several people that Jim MacArthur was Charlie's natural son, not adopted."

I waited while she composed her face.

"Oh, wouldn't that be the most wonderful thing," she said softly.

During the lean years when I was working on the book, Bebe asked me one day, "Would you rather have a Best Seller or be rich?"

"That's easy," I replied. "Best Seller."

Helen was ninety years old when our book was published. It became, overnight, a Best Seller; Helen Hayes was featured in every New York newspaper and magazine, and the morning and evening television programs competed to interview her. One day when we were returning from a book signing in Connecticut, she presented me with a gold commemorative medal bearing her likeness as "First Lady of the Stage." I was touched, but her handwritten note with the medal was the most precious gift:

"Thank you for giving me a last hurrah."

* * *

Three Healers

I have always tried to live my life with enough open spaces to allow unexpected events to come in. I came home from the book excitement in New York and Lara Rivelli was on the phone, breathlessly telling me that "the most famous healer in Europe" was coming to Paraiso in two weeks.

"You must join us. It will be great fun. In Europe, people wait for hours in the sun and the rain just to see a glimpse of the healer, Yvette, but my friends came with her and they'll get us a private audience so we don't have to wait. Please say you'll go."

I didn't know about the "fun" part, but in the interest of broadening my horizons and being a good sport, I agreed to go be healed. I'd had a crick in my neck for a week. Maybe I could get rid of it. It wasn't like I was going to a healer for no reason.

Yvette was making her only North American appearance that year on a soccer field not far from Max's last beauty salon. The field was covered with dry grasses and weeds, and a couple of trees at one end provided the only shade. I had never heard of Yvette, but she was all anyone in Paraiso could talk about as the day of her appearance drew near.

I did know that Mexico is fertile ground for healers. Even before Carlos Castaneda wrote his mystical books that fascinated English-language readers, many people were going to healers down here, much as one would go see a doctor. With Mexico's Indian roots going back thousands of years, it is common, rather than rare, to hear someone talking about going to a healer. Some healers are specialists in ancient methods for healing the body, like putting cauliflower leaves on a tumor to reduce its size, or massaging an arthritic knee with alcohol containing marijuana to ease the stiffness. I hadn't been connected to that network and had no idea how popular it was, but now that the door had been opened by Lara, I was drawn in.

I'd already had a glimmer of what was possible. Near the end of his life, my brother had cancer and, at the urging of friends, he came to see a famous healer in Mexico. The medical doctors in the United States had exhausted treatments for extending his life, but my brother had hope. The healer talked to him for a few minutes, an introduction, and then, without laying a hand on him, focused his powerful spiritual energy on the cancer. My brother and his wife went on vacation in Puerto Vallarta. He lived an additional six months and died with no pain.

The best healers are people with special gifts, mental and spiritual powers carefully nurtured through years of study and practice, which can accomplish results. It doesn't matter if you or I believe in them; whether we believe has no effect on their abilities or success. They believe—know—they have a God-given gift and their lives are dedicated to service to others. That's why many of the best don't charge for what they do.

The day of Yvette's appearance, the streets of Paraiso were full of cars from Mexico City and pedestrians, all heading for the soccer field. Crowds of people chattering with one another streamed by my house shortly after a steamy sunrise and continued all morning. Lara came

THREE HEALERS

about eleven o'clock in her car. Two healers from Tepoztlan, Clay and Ron, were meeting us and we were going together to see Yvette. I greeted them and then Lara said, "It's time to go. The public's allowed in after noon, so if we want to go early, now's the time." As we piled into her car for the short ride, she switched on the air conditioner. The powerful fan blew arctic air for ten minutes and then we were at the field.

Hundreds of people were trampling the dry grass, forming a line under the blazing sun. The line wound around the edges of the soccer field and ended at the foot of a flight of rickety wooden steps with a handrail that led up to a wooden hut on a platform above the crowd. True to her word, Lara delivered us to the head of the line, where we stood for the next thirty minutes. The sun was relentless; not a cloud in the beautiful blue sky.

Suddenly, the man guarding the stairs waved us up. The handrails were full of splinters, but I didn't pause as we hurried single file. At the open door to the hut stood four young women in white. I didn't know what to expect; still, I was surprised to see Yvette's acolytes and was even more curious about Yvette. She had puffy white skin and pale eyes, and appeared to be in her sixties—or maybe twenty or thirty years older than that, it was hard to tell. She wore a long, sheer white dress and sat in a low chair, her feet not quite reaching the wooden floor.

Flies buzzed in the room and there was a smell of mothballs. Lara told me to sit in a chair facing Yvette. Ron and Clay stood quietly.

When I sat down, Yvette gave me a silver medal, as small as a dime and of lighter weight. I thanked her and studied the face of the medal, and asked her what it was, but I don't think she understood my Spanish. She nodded and said something in a low voice. She probably was speaking French. I think the medal was Joan of Arc or St. Christopher or someone from Lourdes. I looked at it with a magnifying glass later but didn't recognize it. I still have it.

Yvette spoke to Lara in a soft voice and Lara nodded at us that it was time to leave. We made our way back down the creaky stairs, passed through the hundreds of sweltering people, and found the car. The driver took us to an attractive adobe house belonging to Lara's cousin, Annette, who happened to be a healer, but not as famous as Yvette.

"Would you like a harmonization?" Annette asked me.

I didn't know what she was talking about. "Oh, Kate, you do," Lara smiled. "It makes you feel wonderful."

I didn't feel bad, but I'd come this far as a good sport. Why quit now? "Sure, OK," I said.

Annette led me to a small bedroom which had twin beds that were neatly made with the spreads pulled up. She told me to lie down on my back on one of the beds. "Leave your clothes on and relax," she said. It was going to be a lot easier to relax in my clothes than without them. She left the room. I closed my eyes.

In a couple of minutes, someone else came into the room. I felt two hands on my abdomen. Hand, hand, left, right. The hands began to move, making small circles. I thought about synchronized swimming. They were large hands, moving very gently. I stopped thinking about swimming and thought about the hands. Large man's hands.

THREE HEALERS

No one had prepared me for that. *What do I do?* I thought. It was too late to disappear as though I'd never been there. The hands paused. I mumbled, "*Muchas gracias,*" squinted at my "harmonizer" and got out.

I found Lara and Annette in the kitchen.

"How was it?" Lara asked. "How did it go? Wasn't it wonderful?"

"It was OK," I said, "but who was that guy rubbing my stomach?"

"**Guy?**" they chorused. "A **guy?**" Lara and Annette looked at each other.

"No idea," Lara said with a shrug, and she began to laugh.

A couple of months later, Bebe called me with the news that Guru Soraya, another healer, was at that moment on her way to Paraiso from Mexico City in her own air-conditioned bus, trailed by scores of excited followers. Did I want to go see her? "Lara is organizing another group," she added.

"Good. I'll go." How far will we go to prove that we're good sports, not stuffy or scared or sissy? Pretty far, I guessed.

Guru Soraya's appearance was well organized. She had leased a hotel for a week of meditation and psycho-cybernetics workshops, and when the doors of the hotel's convention center opened at noon, more than a thousand well-dressed Mexico City women and a few men pushed forward to buy tickets.

I was in their midst feeling definitely underdressed and adrift in Gap in a tossing sea of Chanel. Tickets were expensive, from 250 to 1,250 pesos, about twenty to one hundred dollars, depending on whether one wanted to sit in a front-row chair or watch from the kitchen. I chose halfway and bought a ticket for the tenth row on an aisle. Women in white dresses were selling bouquets of white flowers for faithful followers to present to Guru Soraya. I noticed that those who did not buy flowers did not sit in the first five rows.

The hall was packed and the crowd was becoming restless when Guru Soraya suddenly appeared on a stage through parted curtains. Loud applause met her. She was maybe forty years old, with a perfect figure and a flawless face framed by shining black hair and accented with almond-shaped eyes. Many followers had tiny "Guru Soraya Prayer Rugs" on which they now prostrated themselves. The rest of us knelt on the cement floor with our faces down while Guru Soraya spoke. Her voice was so soft, I could barely hear her.

We each had been given a printed page of the chants in which we were to participate, but I couldn't figure out the language. As it turned out, it didn't matter because they were meditations to do alone, which I did. Part of the session was deep breathing and holding your breath. Every now and then, everyone gave an "Ommmmm" that bounced around in the hall. An hour later, the session was over when Guru Soraya disappeared as suddenly as she had appeared, escorted out of the room by a phalanx of acolytes.

Lara was smiling. "How do you feel?" she asked me.

"I feel fine," I said, "but don't ask my knees how *they* feel."

Neither of the public performances prepared me for Mireya Iturbe, a healer I came to know as a friend; an unassuming, brilliant woman who expanded her

THREE HEALERS

special spiritual powers while she was living a worldly life. She was in her eighties, reading without glasses, drinking her tequila neat, her mind perfectly clear and as comprehensive as her interest in knowing the worlds around her.

Bebe and I invited her for lunch one summer day, and she arrived promptly on time in a beautifully woven Guatemalan blouse, *huipil*, and a long, full skirt of lavender, purple, blue, yellow, and palest rose. Her gentle face was smiling and she wore her silver hair brushed to her shoulders. As she came forward to greet us, a stout carved cane was her only concession to age.

I wanted to know how Mireya discovered she had a gift for healing, and how long ago that was. But first, we were treated to a personal history. Her father, Ramon Fuentes Iturbe, had been the youngest general in the Mexican Revolution. At twenty-one, he delivered a brigade of passionate followers to Francisco I. Madero, his intellectual and spiritual model. In return, Mireya's father received the rank of brigadier general and an army career. Madero was fair, wealthy, and brilliant, she said, the first leader of the Mexican Revolution and the country's first elected president. He was a follower of spiritualism, believing he received messages from his little brother who had died at age four. One such message was: "Be of aid to others." Madero was known as the "Apostle of Democracy," Mireya said, because he tried to lead Mexicans toward freedom, literacy, open elections, an end to slavery, and no reelection. He was assassinated before his goals could be realized.

Mireya had lived an adventurous life. When she was a child, while Mexican leaders were fighting over their country's future, she and her family sought political exile in California, where Mireya learned British English at a convent. After the Revolution, her father became Mexico's military attaché to Japan. The family looked forward to an Oriental adventure, especially Mireya's father, the general, who planned to learn the intricacies of Buddhism, which had always fascinated him.

But when they arrived in Japan in 1940, the United States ambassador met them with an anxious message. "If I were you, General Fuentes, I would send my daughter and wife back to Mexico. We know the Japanese are preparing for war with the United States. We have warned President Roosevelt, but he has not taken steps to prevent a war. Now, on our own, we are sending our women and children away."

Mireya's father passed the news to her mother, who declared she was not going to split the family. "Do you think I'm going to leave you because of a war?" she asked her husband. Mireya's brother went to the United States, where he and his wife had a home, but Mireya and her parents remained in Japan.

"We were on one of the last boats out of Japan," she said. "An earlier boat had turned around and come back, and all of the passengers—mostly American journalists, priests, and businessmen—were put into Japanese concentration camps. We wouldn't have reached the United States if we had taken it."

Three days after the Japanese attacked Hawaii on December 7, 1941, Mexico entered World War II with the Allies and the family was interned as "diplomatic refugees" in the Mexican Embassy in Tokyo. Mireya was eighteen years old, tall and blonde, and having the time of her life. Japanese police and Embassy guards took her and her girlfriends out for a day in a park or for rides around the countryside, while every week or so new rumors flew that the diplomats were going to be sent home "soon."

Finally, the governments of the United States and Japan worked out an exchange of diplomats, and Mireya and her parents prepared to sail from Yokohama. "The guards kept coming into our cabin saying, 'Hurry! You must pack a small bag to take with you. You will be leaving in a few days.' But a week would pass without word of a departure. A month later, a Japanese officer said we would be leaving by ship and could take all of our furniture and other belongings, but not the car. The car was a new Lincoln which my father had bought in San Francisco before leaving for Japan. The Japanese said he couldn't take it back to Mexico, but he could sell it to the Japanese Minister of War for twenty thousand dollars and buy whatever he wanted up to that amount from the Japanese ministry in Tokyo."

Mireya's family chose ivory, pearls, silk brocade, a dozen silk kimonos from which her mother fashioned beautiful dresses, and sets of porcelain dishes. Her mother also bought a Mexican solid silver tea service, made in Mexico and exported to Japan.

At last they were told to board a ship, which sailed back and forth in Yokohama harbor for a week so no one would know when it was leaving. Suddenly, one night in the pitch-black darkness it weighed anchor and they were on their way.

Mireya remembered it well: "Every porthole was full of faces as we cleared the harbor lights and commenced our voyage. There were a lot of journalists on the deck below us, and when they felt the ship moving they came running upstairs, but the Japanese officers wouldn't let them out on deck. They were frantic to see our departure. They ran up and down the corridors, banging on doors, asking if they could use a porthole to see what was happening. Some passengers let them in."

Mireya loved the shipboard life as their vessel traveled under protection of the International Red Cross. All of the young people on board, the children of diplomats, would sit in a big circle in the evenings and sing songs. "Everybody knew I was the daughter of a Mexican general and they thought that was wonderful. We had great fun."

The ship picked up stranded Westerners in Shanghai, where it was halted by a submarine that sailed around it before letting it pass, and in Hong Kong, where many missionaries and priests boarded. The trip ended when they docked in the southeast African neutral Portuguese colony of Lourenco Marques—now Maputo, Mozambique—for an official exchange of diplomats and their families.

"The other ship was already there," Mireya related, her voice brimming with excitement at the memory. "It had brought Japanese, German, and Italian diplomats from New York and Washington, and would take us to

THREE HEALERS

America. Everyone was out on deck on both ships—finally going home!—and we all began shouting back and forth, trying to catch up on the news. We had been completely out of touch, and do you know what everyone wanted to know? Who was ahead in the baseball season! Once we boarded the *Gripsholm,* we were on our way. When we reached New York, we bought another new car and drove to Mexico."

In Mexico, Mireya was the first person to receive an English Studies proficiency diploma from Cambridge University of England; she was tested and passed in the inaugural year of the British Council in Mexico City. She became an English teacher at the Anglo-Mexican Institute in Mexico City, because she wanted to improve her own English, and she also developed into a talented painter.

At age fifty-eight, she realized her special talent—psycho-cybernetics, the ability to heal by natural cosmic energy—which is being taught now in some medical schools as a recognized force. All religions use it, as well as long-distance visualization. The energy goes where it is focused, like a laser beam.

"A healer in Mexico City came to Cuernavaca to heal a friend of mine," Mireya said. "The friend's husband was a gynecologist, and my friend had leukemia. The healer was Santiago Flores, a spiritual healer who gave lectures on healing. I had never met him, but I was in a group that meditated once a week and he invited our group to his next lectures. It turned out that the only people at his lecture were members of the group I was in.

"He asked if anyone needed a healing and I said I did. I had been diagnosed by doctors with endometrial cancer. Santiago gave me a healing that day, and afterward he said, 'You don't have cancer.'

"I told my friends in Mexico City what had happened and they insisted I go to a very highly thought-of oncologist. I went and saw him, and after a week of examinations and tests, he said, 'You do not have cancer.'

"I was delighted. I wondered how Santiago could have known this when it had taken the oncologist a week to figure it out. I called Santiago and he put me in contact with Sergio Gonzalez de la Garza, a brilliant man who gave seminars on healing.

"For the next twenty years, I went to seminar after seminar. Then, a group of us who had been studying together received permission to work at healing patients in a Cuernavaca nursing home, to practice what we had been learning. Everyone at the home was very respectful of us and pleased that we wanted to help them. We had good results."

Mireya went to Guatemala to learn about other healing practices, and while there she fell in love with Mario Monteforte, one of Guatemala's most accomplished novelists, a prominent politician, and a celebrated poet and essayist. They were married, but it didn't take long for both to realize that, as much as they loved each other, they could not live together in harmony. Mireya returned to Cuernavaca. Upon Mario's death in 2003, the president of Guatemala decreed three days of national mourning.

THREE HEALERS

Like many of the most accomplished healers, Mireya never charged a cent. She successfully treated and healed patients who came to her with bad equilibrium, poor circulation, coughs, severe colds, arthritis, diabetes, faulty vision, pain, high blood pressure, heart palpitations, or were having a bad day and just wanted to hear one of Mireya's fascinating stories.

* * *

Last Call

On the day that the world was supposed to end, my biggest immediate problem was deciding what to wear. Ordinarily, I don't care what I wear, but this was obviously a special occasion due to the possibility of no tomorrow, so if I was going to change my mind, I had to do it quickly and, you might say, permanently. I didn't want to look too casual. I guessed that my Mexican friends and neighbors were rolling out their finest frocks and jewelry for this ultimate appearance, but I had trouble convincing myself that the world was really going to end.

It had all started when I visited the London Planetarium that summer of 1979 and learned that something bad might happen to me. Specifically, the planets were going to line up, something they had never done before, and even the astronomers who had royal titles and letters after their names were uncertain what might happen. An announcer with a deep, tremulous voice told the audience in the darkened Planetarium, "We don't know what might happen next! ALL HELL COULD BREAK LOOSE!"

I had a vision of the planets lining up in a row like the Rockettes and civilization running for the exits. Then the lights came on and we shuffled out of the theater, blinking in the sunshine and wondering what was real. I returned to Mexico and thought no more about it. I put it out of my mind, or so I thought.

SUDDENLY, MEXICO!

Lara Rivelli invited me to an end-of-the-world party at her estate on the night the planets were supposed to be lining up. It was sure to be an international mix of lively people—artists, intellectuals, diplomats, healers and psychics, gurus, musicians—anyone who interested her.

"The party will be perfect at my house because all of my old magnolia trees are at the sides of the garden," she said. "If there are earthquakes, nothing will fall on us. I'm inviting everyone, and there will be plenty to eat and drink. If this is our last night, I want everyone to have fun."

So here I was, dressing for what might be the last party EVER! and there was no dress code. I decided to stay with black; it was easy. A black silk outfit of slacks and a shirt, with shoes I could kick off in case I had to run for my life. From what? Boulders falling out of the sky? Torrential rain and lightning? Earthquakes? Mud slides? The silk was washable; I didn't want to ruin good clothes.

As I was leaving my house for the party, the phone rang. I grabbed it and was happy to hear Phil Bangsberg, my editor at the *South China Morning Post* in Hong Kong. He asked if I had finished an assignment he had given me. I told him I had and he said, "Good girl" or something like that, and that's when I had my idea.

"Phil, are you in Hong Kong?" I asked.

"Yes. I'm at the office."

"What time is it? Is it tomorrow?"

"Your tomorrow? Yes."

"I'm on my way to an end-of-the-world party and I'm relieved to know the world hasn't ended yet over there. Thanks."

There was a puzzled pause. "No, we're all still here." Another pause. "Well, have a good time, then. Cheerio!"

Guests were strolling in Lara's garden and a big group was clustered near the bar when I arrived. I waved at Diego and Santiago, both casually dressed, and saw Madame Natalia stalking through the crowd in a silver bat-wing cape. I hugged Lara and shook hands with the man she was talking to, a very polite businessman from Japan. I told them about my call from Hong Kong and that the world had not ended yet.

"Oh, darling, I never worry about things like that," Lara said. "I just thought the end of the world was a perfect excuse for a party."

The world didn't end and I'm still here...stay tuned.

※ ※ ※

Stroke Of Luck

Bebe entered the real estate business by a stroke of luck. A successful older broker wanted to retire and persuaded her to take over the business, giving Bebe a running start. Then she found a small, charming Mexican Colonial bungalow covered in bright pink bougainvillea and sold it to me! It was her first sale, and for me, the house was love at first sight. Bebe said I had brought her good luck.

Lara decided to return to her home in Portofino and asked Bebe to handle that sale. Bebe was conflicted: she didn't want Lara to leave Paraiso, but if Lara's mind was made up, Bebe wanted to be the person to sell her property. Lara promised Bebe a double commission to sell the dramatic estate and Bebe went right to work.

A Japanese businessman we had met at Lara's end-of-the-world party was the first potential buyer. He said he would pay the full asking price if Lara would include hundreds of white butterflies he had seen fluttering in her garden. I offered to catch them in a burlap bag to seal the deal, but unfortunately, the client died of a heart attack before he could buy. At the time, Japanese men rarely suffered fatal heart attacks.

Bebe's next serious client was a California oilman whose only requirement was a helipad for his personal helicopter. There was plenty of room for it in the lower garden, Bebe told him. He happily wrote a check for the deposit on the estate and drove away in his long, shiny automobile. But the price of oil took a nosedive and he had to walk away from the property—and his deposit.

SUDDENLY, MEXICO!

The following Friday, Bebe showed the estate to an attractive, well-dressed couple that fell in love with it and wanted to buy it immediately, but they had made a tentative offer on another house and had to wait until that offer was accepted or rejected.

On Saturday, Bebe received word that our dear friend Lara had died in Portofino. Her stepchildren swarmed into Mexico; by Sunday, their moving vans were parked at the Paraiso estate, where they had already raised the price of the house and reduced the commission for the seller. The stepdaughters were straight out of "Cinderella," spoiled grown women constantly quarrelling, each with her own office and corps of lawyers and hangers-on. Bebe remained calm and patiently hauled everyone to lawyers' offices. In the end, she sold the estate to the nice couple, who remained her lifelong friends.

A client known as "The Spaniard" came into Bebe's life when he bought a small house in Paraiso for his mistress, "Anita." The Spaniard was giving Anita a new car for every week they were together, and Anita's entourage, besides The Spaniard, consisted of an ex-husband, her boyfriend, her Italian lover (who was in the state penitentiary for fraud), and her personal staff of cook, butler, maid, and chauffeur. The Spaniard's wife lived in a condominium with the children.

One day, The Spaniard saw a beautiful house he wanted to give to Anita. It was a three-story mansion with an atrium, elevator, swimming pool, exotic gardens, and a master suite that looked like a sheik's tent, only bigger and without the camels.

The Spaniard was captivated, and insisted Anita and Bebe escort him every day while he measured the enormous rooms, inspected the luxurious furnishings, and enjoyed the views of the tropical landscape. When he wanted to see the house at night, Bebe and Anita watched in fear as he pulled a pistol out of his pocket and emptied it at the sky.

It was perhaps inevitable that Anita and The Spaniard had a big blowup when he took back the cars—which, it turned out, he had only leased for her. He ordered the chauffeur to pack his clothes and he drove away. Watching him depart, Anita's ex-husband told her that he would buy the big house for her if she would return to him. Anita's Italian lover called her on his cellular phone and said The Spaniard would "never, never" buy her the big house because he was only staying with Anita to hide from people he had cheated.

Then the Italian lover said, "Anita, if you will come back to me, I will buy that house for you."

He invited her to share champagne and caviar with him at eight o'clock that evening in his suite at the penitentiary, and to spend the night. His butler would meet her at the gate and escort her inside. Anita accepted.

Then there was "Joe Boston" (or whatever his real name was), a cocky guy who called Bebe several times a day on her cell phone, beginning around late August 2001, when he first inquired about buying a house in Mexico. He said he was the grandson of a Mafioso and had three billion dollars in a bank. He lived in New England, he told her, but he wanted to "change his life" and move his family to Mexico.

He sounded nice, Bebe said, and serious about wanting to move his family. She told him what she had for sale in Cuernavaca; he liked best a furnished Mexican Colonial mansion on tree-covered acreage with seventeen bedrooms and a stable. He said he planned to add a wing to the enormous house, and that he was coming to Mexico with twenty-one members of his family.

"Joe" wanted to know if there was space in Acapulco to moor his oceangoing sailboat—which, it turned out, was longer than the port's cruise-ship berth. He also said his wife was pregnant and that she would need a midwife. Could Bebe hire one for her? Of course.

Because it would take about six weeks to close on the property he wanted, "Joe" would come to Mexico to rent a villa for his immediate family and another large house for his bodyguards and the dogs.

"Joe" and his family were going to fly to Cuernavaca on a certain date, landing at the resort's small airport where they would be picked up by vans at twelve o'clock. Bebe didn't know if "Joe" meant twelve o'clock noon or midnight, so she called the telephone number he had given to her to contact him in New England. No one answered. She tried the number he had given her for his mother's home in Florida. No one answered. She called both numbers repeatedly, from noon to midnight, but "Joe Boston" never answered, nor did anyone else. He was a no-show. Bebe paid all the expenses of the waiting chauffeurs.

The next day, still within the "no fly" period imposed by the U.S. government following 9/11, Bebe began wondering about "Joe." Who was he?

In the following months and years, possible clues appeared on the Internet:

STROKE OF LUCK

By Kevin Cullen: "Bin Laden Kin Flown Back to Saudi Arabia." *The Boston Globe*, 20 September 2001. By Eric Lichtblau: "White House Approved Departure of Saudis After Sept. 11, Ex-Aide Says." *The New York Times*, 4 September 2003.

Bebe guessed that "Joe" never got his new life.

✷ ✷ ✷

Heart To Heart

When a gigantic earthquake crushed Mexico's beautiful little neighbor Guatemala in 1976, Mexicans responded from their hearts. It was a far cry from the "monthly payroll deduction" way of giving, like in some countries, as teams of Mexican physicians and disaster specialists raced overland for Central America. Radio stations constantly broadcast calls for donations of clothing and canned goods and people responded, with mountains of help pouring into hastily designated collection centers in town squares and state capitals. Paraiso radio announcers said trucks were leaving from the state capitol every afternoon that week, and people should go there with donations.

The capitol sits on our main plaza, a formal, rather austere structure. I telephoned Bebe, and she and her children were already cleaning out closets and toy boxes. We drove to the capitol.

A red tractor trailer was parked squarely in front of the building's open doors. The top of the trailer was covered with a canvas tarpaulin, held down with ropes, and as we drew near, we could read a big banner stretched across the hood: "Help from the People of Mexico to the People of Guatemala."

The truck's motor was idling with a loud rattling as we swerved in front of it and stopped. Ours was the only car. We grabbed our sacks, threw open the car doors and leaped out to run to the trailer. A man sitting up on top of it loosened the tarp and opened a small space on one side. We could see that the truck was full, but he pushed aside sacks and boxes to make room for our donations and we pitched them up to him, one at a time. He stuffed them into the space he'd made, and then he smoothed out the tarp to cover everything, pulled it taut, and tied it down. He climbed down the back of the rig while we shouted our thanks, and he waved as he stepped up into the passenger side of the cab. The driver gunned the motor and the truck drove away, heading for Guatemala.

Since that day, there have been many trucks from the Mexican people delivering help to the victims of other earthquakes in Mexico and its small neighbors. With the new century, banks began opening special accounts to benefit the victims of natural disasters—earthquakes, hurricanes, tropical storms—and running advertisements in national newspapers, explaining how to make a contribution. But we still go through our closets and game chests and kitchen cabinets to find what we can. We always find something and the big red trucks still leave, headed for wherever people have lost everything but hope.

Things have changed only slightly since that Guatemalan quake. The last time we gave, a huge, bright red Coca-Cola truck was loaded to haul hastily filled boxes and sacks of bottled water and clothing, precious toys and canned goods to victims of the newest catastrophe. In many countries, those red trucks are a more familiar sight than the national flag, but this was no commercial mission. Covering the hood was a banner with the proud, heartfelt message: "From the People of Mexico!"

* * *

Something Like Woof! Woof!

Criticism of a Mexican president was against the law until a few years ago. Not even newspaper cartoonists could safely punch holes in the chief executive's self-proclaimed sanctity. Such treatment was the result of one political party's domination of the country for more than seventy years. Almost everyone was affiliated with the PRI, the Institutional Revolutionary Party, which ran the country. That ended in 2000 with the creation of new opposition political parties.

People in Mexico don't expect much from their politicians, but in extreme cases an errant officeholder may be punished in an unusual way.

While the criticism ban was still in place and the economy was wobbling, the president tried to dodge blame for the situation when he declared publicly that he would defend the Mexican peso "like a dog." He soon presided over a devaluation of the peso which bankrupt thousands of businesses, threw millions out of work, and drastically diminished the quality of everyone's life.

But the Mexican people took delicious revenge: they barked like dogs.

Every place the president went, people barked at him. Some called "Arf! Arf!" Others howled or yipped. The barking sounds followed him throughout the land, and there was nothing he could do about it.

※ ※ ※

Now And Then

Mexico is a place of immense distances, great heights, vast oceans, and far horizons; of skyscrapers and super-highways and sleek underground trains. It has the Atlantic Ocean and the Pacific Ocean, the Gulf of Mexico and the Caribbean Sea. Had it not sold off a large chunk of useless property in 1848, it's a good bet it probably would be its own continent by now. Still, it remains rooted in small-town village life, the life of the pueblos, where rich and poor snack side by side at their favorite taco stands and dance in the street at the village fiestas.

For a look into the heart of the Mexican people, leave the highways and follow a country road to a pueblo. Find the *zócalo* and there you will discover the life of the people. There will be a streetlight, a few stone or iron benches, and a big tree. During the day, the *zócalo* becomes the World Cup stadium for little boys in hand-me-down clothes, kicking a scuffed soccer ball, proud of their speed and their sweat, and running as hard as they can.

A balloon vendor may take his place in the shade of the tree. He wears faded overalls and a straw hat and goes about his work methodically, carefully separating the string of the one balloon chosen by a child from the sea of balls bobbing above her head, shutting out the sky. As the man passes the string to the waiting child, she smiles as though she cannot believe the gift is hers.

The *zócalo* is the living room for people who don't have a living room, a place where dreams are dreamed and sometimes come true. A young couple, teenagers, sit next to one another on a stone bench, speaking softly, laughing. They share furtive kisses until the sun is setting and it is time to reluctantly return to a dreary room in a parents' tiny house. It is hard to be alone after being with the one you love. Far from reaching their dreams, they listen alone to the love songs in their heads.

On Sunday morning, a band plays in the *zócalo* and people wear their best clothes to listen. Vendors stroll among them, offering pink cotton candy and little paper cones filled with slices of mango, papaya, and pineapple. A village woman sets up a stand to sell tamales and the aroma of sweet *masa* drifts on the air, while a shoeshine man polishes the boots of farmers who wouldn't want to be seen on a street in dusty boots.

In the long shadows of evening, an old man sits quietly on a bench beneath the laurel tree and faces the fading sun. Parents with small children stroll to greet him in warm tones, calling him *Abuelito*, dear grandfather. At sixty, he is the oldest man in the village and its historian.

In these smallest villages, an inhabitant will assume the role of keeping history alive, telling the stories of brave men and beautiful women, runaway horses and glorious battles that passed through this poor, sleepy village a long time ago. Where a village is too small to have a school, its inhabitants learn their history from the *Abuelito*.

Neighbors settle themselves on benches around him while children sit cross-legged on the ground and babies are held wrapped and sleeping in their parents' arms. The *Abuelito* clears his throat and all hold a little breath they have been saving for this moment. Only when everyone is still does the *Abuelito* begin to speak.

"*Habia una vez*," he begins. "Once upon a time," and he spins a tale none of them will ever forget.

* * *

The Shepherd

Once long ago, as I drove to Mexico City on the old highway from Laredo, I saw a shepherd sitting on a grassy hillside with his sheep scattered around him across the crown of the hill. He was a teenager, maybe younger, and was facing the highway, sitting there without a hat and holding a small transistor radio to one ear. Transistor radios had only recently become popular in Mexico, and when I saw that boy listening to somewhere else, I thought, "This is the end of Mexico as I know it."

Over the years, I have thought of that shepherd and what was happening to Mexico, and I think now that I was both right and wrong. The transistor radio opened the world to isolated people, but for many of them the old ways haven't disappeared. The small towns, so picturesque and charming, are still here.

While many in Mexico are connected by phones and cars and the Internet, a great multitude continue to live one-dimensional lives. They will never drive a car. They will never live in a house with indoor plumbing. They will never finish the sixth grade. This is the tragedy of Mexico, and the great hope. Maybe tomorrow will be better. "*Tal vez, mañana.*"

Progress has come to Paraiso, but it remains paradise.

THE END

* * *